SMOKE AND STEEL

BY

CARL SANDBURG

Author of " Chicago Poems,"
" Cornhuskers "

NEW YORK

HARCOURT, BRACE AND COMPANY

PRINTED IN THE U. S. A.

THE QUINN & BODEN COMPANY
RAHWAY, N. J

To

COL. EDWARD J. STEICHEN

PAINTER OF NOCTURNES AND FACES, CAMERA ENGRAVER
OF GLINTS AND MOMENTS, LISTENER TO BLUE
EVENING WINDS AND NEW YELLOW ROSES,
DREAMER AND FINDER, RIDER OF GREAT
MORNINGS IN GARDENS, VALLEYS,
BATTLES.

Acknowledgments are due *Poetry* (Chicago), *The New Republic, The Liberator, The Dial,* and *The Chicago Daily News* for permission to reprint poems that appeared originally in their pages.

CONTENTS

Contents vii

SMOKE NIGHTS

SMOKE AND STEEL

SMOKE of the fields in spring is one,
Smoke of the leaves in autumn another.
Smoke of a steel-mill roof or a battleship funnel,
They all go up in a line with a smokestack,
Or they twist . . . in the slow twist . . . of the wind.

If the north wind comes they run to the south.
If the west wind comes they run to the east.
        By this sign
        all smokes
        know each other.
Smoke of the fields in spring and leaves in autumn,
Smoke of the finished steel, chilled and blue,
By the oath of work they swear: " I know you."

Hunted and hissed from the center
Deep down long ago when God made us over,
Deep down are the cinders we came from—
You and I and our heads of smoke.

        . . . .

Some of the smokes God dropped on the job
Cross on the sky and count our years
And sing in the secrets of our numbers;
Sing their dawns and sing their evenings,
Sing an old log-fire song:

You may put the damper up,
You may put the damper down,
The smoke goes up the chimney just the same.

Smoke of a city sunset skyline,
Smoke of a country dusk horizon—
They cross on the sky and count our years.

. . . .

Smoke of a brick-red dust
Winds on a spiral
Out of the stacks
For a hidden and glimpsing moon.
This, said the bar-iron shed to the blooming mill,
This is the slang of coal and steel.
The day-gang hands it to the night-gang,
The night-gang hands it back.

Stammer at the slang of this—
Let us understand half of it.
In the rolling mills and sheet mills,
In the harr and boom of the blast fires,
The smoke changes its shadow
And men change their shadow;
A nigger, a wop, a bohunk changes.

A bar of steel—it is only
Smoke at the heart of it, smoke and the blood of a man.
A runner of fire ran in it, ran out, ran somewhere else,
And left—smoke and the blood of a man
And the finished steel, chilled and blue.

So fire runs in, runs out, runs somewhere else again,
And the bar of steel is a gun, a wheel, a nail, a shovel,
A rudder under the sea, a steering-gear in the sky;
And always dark in the heart and through it,
> Smoke and the blood of a man.
Pittsburg, Youngstown, Gary—they make their steel
> with men.

In the blood of men and the ink of chimneys
The smoke nights write their oaths:
Smoke into steel and blood into steel;
Homestead, Braddock, Birmingham, they make their
> steel with men.
Smoke and blood is the mix of steel.

> The birdmen drone
> in the blue; it is steel
> a motor sings and zooms.

. . . .

Steel barb-wire around The Works.
Steel guns in the holsters of the guards at the gates of
> The Works.
Steel ore-boats bring the loads clawed from the earth
> by steel, lifted and lugged by arms of steel, sung
> on its way by the clanking clam-shells.
The runners now, the handlers now, are steel; they dig
> and clutch and haul; they hoist their automatic
> knuckles from job to job; they are steel making
> steel.

Fire and dust and air fight in the furnaces; the pour is
     timed, the billets wriggle; the clinkers are dumped:
Liners on the sea, skyscrapers on the land; diving steel
     in the sea, climbing steel in the sky.

. . . .

Finders in the dark, you Steve with a dinner bucket,
     you Steve clumping in the dusk on the sidewalks
     with an evening paper for the woman and kids,
     you Steve with your head wondering where we
     all end up—
Finders in the dark, Steve: I hook my arm in cinder
     sleeves; we go down the street together; it is all
     the same to us; you Steve and the rest of us end
     on the same stars; we all wear a hat in hell
     together, in hell or heaven.

Smoke nights now, Steve.
Smoke, smoke, lost in the sieves of yesterday;
Dumped again to the scoops and hooks today.
Smoke like the clocks and whistles, always.
     Smoke nights now.
     To-morrow something else.

. . . .

Luck moons come and go:
Five men swim in a pot of red steel.
Their bones are kneaded into the bread of steel:
Their bones are knocked into coils and anvils
And the sucking plungers of sea-fighting turbines.
Look for them in the woven frame of a wireless station.

So ghosts hide in steel like heavy-armed men in
  mirrors.
Peepers, skulkers—they shadow-dance in laughing
  tombs.
They are always there and they never answer.

One of them said: "I like my job, the company is
  good to me, America is a wonderful country."
One: "Jesus, my bones ache; the company is a liar;
  this is a free country, like hell."
One: "I got a girl, a peach; we save up and go on a
  farm and raise pigs and be the boss ourselves."
And the others were roughneck singers a long ways
  from home.
Look for them back of a steel vault door.

> They laugh at the cost.
> They lift the birdmen into the blue.
> It is steel a motor sings and zooms.

In the subway plugs and drums,
In the slow hydraulic drills, in gumbo or gravel,
Under dynamo shafts in the webs of armature spiders,
They shadow-dance and laugh at the cost.

. . . .

The ovens light a red dome.
Spools of fire wind and wind.
Quadrangles of crimson sputter.
The lashes of dying maroon let down.
Fire and wind wash out the slag.
Forever the slag gets washed in fire and wind.

The anthem learned by the steel is:
>   Do this or go hungry.
Look for our rust on a plow.
Listen to us in a threshing-engine razz.
Look at our job in the running wagon wheat.

. . . .

Fire and wind wash at the slag.
Box-cars, clocks, steam-shovels, churns, pistons, boilers,
>   scissors—
Oh, the sleeping slag from the mountains, the slag-
>   heavy pig-iron will go down many roads.
Men will stab and shoot with it, and make butter and
>   tunnel rivers, and mow hay in swaths, and slit
>   hogs and skin beeves, and steer airplanes across
>   North America, Europe, Asia, round the world.

Hacked from a hard rock country, broken and baked
>   in mills and smelters, the rusty dust waits
Till the clean hard weave of its atoms cripples and
>   blunts the drills chewing a hole in it.
The steel of its plinths and flanges is reckoned, O God,
>   in one-millionth of an inch.

. . . .

Once when I saw the curves of fire, the rough scarf
>   women dancing,
Dancing out of the flues and smoke-stacks—flying hair
>   of fire, flying feet upside down;
Buckets and baskets of fire exploding and chortling,
>   fire running wild out of the steady and fastened
>   ovens;

Sparks cracking a harr-harr-huff from a solar-plexus
    of rock-ribs of the earth taking a laugh for them-
    selves;
Ears and noses of fire, gibbering gorilla arms of fire,
    gold mud-pies, gold bird-wings, red jackets riding
    purple mules, scarlet autocrats tumbling from the
    humps of camels, assassinated czars straddling
    vermillion balloons;
I saw then the fires flash one by one: good-by: then
    smoke, smoke;
And in the screens the great sisters of night and cool
    stars, sitting women arranging their hair,
Waiting in the sky, waiting with slow easy eyes, wait-
    ing and half-murmuring:
      "Since you know all
      and I know nothing,
      tell me what I dreamed last night."

    . . . .

Pearl cobwebs in the windy rain,
in only a flicker of wind,
are caught and lost and never known again.

A pool of moonshine comes and waits,
but never waits long: the wind picks up
loose gold like this and is gone.

A bar of steel sleeps and looks slant-eyed
on the pearl cobwebs, the pools of moonshine;
sleeps slant-eyed a million years,

sleeps with a coat of rust, a vest of moths,
a shirt of gathering sod and loam.

The wind never bothers . . . a bar of steel.
The wind picks only . . pearl cobwebs . . pools
of moonshine.

FIVE TOWNS ON THE B. AND O.

By day . . . tireless smokestacks . . . hungry smoky
   shanties hanging to the slopes . . . crooning:
   We get by, that's all.
By night . . . all lit up . . . fire-gold bars, fire-gold
   flues . . . and the shanties shaking in clumsy
   shadows . . . almost the hills shaking . . . all
   crooning: By God, we're going to find out or
   know why.

WORK GANGS

Box cars run by a mile long.
And I wonder what they say to each other
When they stop a mile long on a sidetrack.
        Maybe their chatter goes:
I came from Fargo with a load of wheat up to the
        danger line.
I came from Omaha with a load of shorthorns and
        they splintered my boards.
I came from Detroit heavy with a load of flivvers.
I carried apples from the Hood river last year and this
        year bunches of bananas from Florida; they look
        for me with watermelons from Mississippi next
        year.

Hammers and shovels of work gangs sleep in shop
        corners
when the dark stars come on the sky and the night
        watchmen walk and look.

Then the hammer heads talk to the handles,
then the scoops of the shovels talk,
how the day's work nicked and trimmed them,
how they swung and lifted all day,
how the hands of the work gangs smelled of hope.

In the night of the dark stars
when the curve of the sky is a work gang handle,
in the night on the mile long sidetracks,
in the night where the hammers and shovels sleep in
    corners,
the night watchmen stuff their pipes with dreams—
and sometimes they doze and don't care for nothin',
and sometimes they search their heads for meanings,
    stories, stars.
      The stuff of it runs like this:
A long way we come; a long way to go; long rests and
    long deep sniffs for our lungs on the way.
Sleep is a belonging of all; even if all songs are old
    songs and the singing heart is snuffed out like a
    switchman's lantern with the oil gone, even if we
    forget our names and houses in the finish, the
    secret of sleep is left us, sleep belongs to all,
    sleep is the first and last and best of all.

People singing; people with song mouths connecting
    with song hearts; people who must sing or die;
    people whose song hearts break if there is no
    song mouth; these are my people.

PENNSYLVANIA

I HAVE been in Pennsylvania,
In the Monongahela and the Hocking Valleys.

In the blue Susquehanna
On a Saturday morning
I saw the mounted constabulary go by,
I saw boys playing marbles.
Spring and the hills laughed.

And in places
Along the Appalachian chain,
I saw steel arms handling coal and iron,
And I saw the white-cauliflower faces
Of miners' wives waiting for the men to come home
    from the day's work.

I made color studies in crimson and violet
Over the dust and domes of culm at sunset.

WHIRLS

NEITHER rose leaves gathered in a jar—respectably in
Boston—these—nor drops of Christ blood for a
chalice—decently in Philadelphia or Baltimore.

Cinders—these—hissing in a marl and lime of Chicago
—also these—the howling of northwest winds
across North and South Dakota—or the spatter
of winter spray on sea rocks of Kamchatka.

PEOPLE WHO MUST

PEOPLE WHO MUST

I PAINTED on the roof of a skyscraper.
I painted a long while and called it a day's work.
The people on a corner swarmed and the traffic cop's
    whistle never let up all afternoon.
They were the same as bugs, many bugs on their way—
Those people on the go or at a standstill;
And the traffic cop a spot of blue, a splinter of brass,
Where the black tides ran around him
And he kept the street. I painted a long while
And called it a day's work.

ALLEY RATS

THEY were calling certain styles of whiskers by the
    name of " lilacs."
And another manner of beard assumed in their chatter
    a verbal guise
Of " mutton chops," " galways," " feather dusters."

Metaphors such as these sprang from their lips while
    other street cries
Sprang from sparrows finding scattered oats among
    interstices of the curb.
Ah-hah these metaphors—and Ah-hah these boys—
    among the police they were known
As the Dirty Dozen and their names took the front
    pages of newspapers
And two of them croaked on the same day at a " neck-
    tie party " .·. . if we employ the metaphors of
    their lips.

ELEVENTH AVENUE RACKET

THERE is something terrible
about a hurdy-gurdy,
a gipsy man and woman,
and a monkey in red flannel
all stopping in front of a big house
with a sign " For Rent " on the door
and the blinds hanging loose
and nobody home.
I never saw this.
I hope to God I never will.

Whoop-de-doodle-de-doo.
Hoodle-de-harr-de-hum.
Nobody home? Everybody home.
Whoop-de-doodle-de-doo.
Mamie Riley married Jimmy Higgins last night: Eddie
Jones died of whooping cough: George Hacks got
a job on the police force: the Rosenheims bought
a brass bed: Lena Hart giggled at a jackie: a
pushcart man called to*may*toes, to*may*toes.
Whoop-de-doodle-de-doo.
Hoodle-de-harr-de-hum.
Nobody home? Everybody home.

HOME FIRES

In a Yiddish eating place on Rivington Street . . .
    faces . . . coffee spots . . . children kicking at
    the night stars with bare toes from bare buttocks.
They know it is September on Rivington when the red
    tomaytoes cram the pushcarts,
Here the children snozzle at milk bottles, children who
    have never seen a cow.
Here the stranger wonders how so many people re-
    member where they keep home fires.

HATS

HATS, where do you belong?
        what is under you?

On the rim of a skyscraper's forehead
I looked down and saw: hats: fifty thousand hats:
Swarming with a noise of bees and sheep, cattle and
        waterfalls,
Stopping with a silence of sea grass, a silence of
        prairie corn.
        Hats: tell me your high hopes.

THEY ALL WANT TO PLAY HAMLET

THEY all want to play Hamlet.
They have not exactly seen their fathers killed
Nor their mothers in a frame-up to kill,
Nor an Ophelia dying with a dust gagging the heart,
Not exactly the spinning circles of singing golden
    spiders,
Not exactly this have they got at nor the meaning of
    flowers—O flowers, flowers slung by a dancing
    girl—in the saddest play the inkfish, Shakespeare,
    ever wrote;
Yet they all want to play Hamlet because it is sad
    like all actors are sad and to stand by an open
    grave with a joker's skull in the hand and then
    to say over slow and say over slow wise, keen,
    beautiful words masking a heart that's breaking,
    breaking,
This is something that calls and calls to their blood.
They are acting when they talk about it and they know
    it is acting to be particular about it and yet: They
    all want to play Hamlet.

THE MAYOR OF GARY

I ASKED the Mayor of Gary about the 12-hour day and the 7-day week.

And the Mayor of Gary answered more workmen steal time on the job in Gary than any other place in the United States.

"Go into the plants and you will see men sitting around doing nothing—machinery does everything," said the Mayor of Gary when I asked him about the 12-hour day and the 7-day week.

And he wore cool cream pants, the Mayor of Gary, and white shoes, and a barber had fixed him up with a shampoo and a shave and he was easy and imperturbable though the government weather bureau thermometer said 96 and children were soaking their heads at bubbling fountains on the street corners.

And I said good-by to the Mayor of Gary and I went out from the city hall and turned the corner into Broadway.

And I saw workmen wearing leather shoes scruffed with fire and cinders, and pitted with little holes from running molten steel,

And some had bunches of specialized muscles around their shoulder blades hard as pig iron, muscles of their fore-arms were sheet steel and they looked to me like men who had been somewhere.

Gary, Indiana, 1915.

OMAHA

RED barns and red heifers spot the green
grass circles around Omaha—the farmers
haul tanks of cream and wagon loads of
cheese.

Shale hogbacks across the river at Council
Bluffs—and shanties hang by an eyelash to
the hill slants back around Omaha.

A span of steel ties up the kin of Iowa and
Nebraska across the yellow, big-hoofed Missouri
River.

Omaha, the roughneck, feeds armies,
Eats and swears from a dirty face.
Omaha works to get the world a breakfast.

GALOOTS

GALOOTS, you hairy, hankering,
Snousle on the bones you eat, chew at the gristle and
lick the last of it.
Grab off the bones in the paws of other galoots—hook
your claws in their sleazy mouths—snap and run.
If long-necks sit on their rumps and sing wild cries
to the winter moon, chasing their tails to the
flickers of foolish stars . . . let 'em howl.
Galoots fat with too much, galoots lean with too little,
galoot millions and millions, snousle and snicker
on, plug your exhausts, hunt your snacks of fat
and lean, grab off yours.

CRABAPPLE BLOSSOMS

Somebody's little girl—how easy to make a sob
story over who she was once and who she is
now.
Somebody's little girl—she played once under a crabapple tree in June and the blossoms fell on the
dark hair.

It was somewhere on the Erie line and the town was
Salamanca or Painted Post or Horse's Head.
And out of her hair she shook the blossoms and went
into the house and her mother washed her face
and her mother had an ache in her heart at a rebel
voice, " I don't want to."

Somebody's little girl—forty little girls of somebodies
splashed in red tights forming horseshoes, arches,
pyramids—forty little show girls, ponies, squabs.
How easy a sob story over who she once was and who
she is now—and how the crabapple blossoms fell
on her dark hair in June.

Let the lights of Broadway spangle and splatter—and
the taxis hustle the crowds away when the show
is over and the street goes dark.

Let the girls wash off the paint and go for their midnight sandwiches—let 'em dream in the morning
 sun, late in the morning, long after the morning
 papers and the milk wagons—
Let 'em dream long as they want to . . . of June
 somewhere on the Erie line . . . and crabapple
 blossoms.

REAL ESTATE NEWS

ARMOUR AVENUE was the name of this street and door
    signs on empty houses read " The Silver Dollar,"
    " Swede Annie " and the Christian names of
    madams such as " Myrtle " and " Jenny."
Scrap iron, rags and bottles fill the front rooms hither
    and yon and signs in Yiddish say Abe Kaplan &
    Co. are running junk shops in whore houses of
    former times.
The segregated district, the Tenderloin, is here no
    more; the red-lights are gone; the ring of shovels
    handling scrap iron replaces the banging of pianos
    and the bawling songs of pimps.
Chicago, 1915.

MANUAL SYSTEM

MARY has a thingamajig clamped on her ears
And sits all day taking plugs out and sticking plugs in.
Flashes and flashes—voices and voices
                        calling for ears to pour words in
Faces at the ends of wires asking for other faces
                        at the ends of other wires:
All day taking plugs out and sticking plugs in,
Mary has a thingamajig clamped on her ears.

STRIPES

POLICEMAN in front of a bank 3 A.M. . . . lonely.
Policeman State and Madison . . . high noon . . .
    mobs . . . cars . . . parcels . . . lonely.

Woman in suburbs . . . keeping night watch on a
    sleeping typhoid patient . . . only a clock to talk
    to . . . lonesome.
Woman selling gloves . . . bargain day department
    store . . . furious crazy-work of many hands
    slipping in and out of gloves . . . lonesome.

HONKY TONK IN CLEVELAND, OHIO

It's a jazz affair, drum crashes and cornet razzes.
The trombone pony neighs and the tuba jackass snorts.
The banjo tickles and titters too awful.
The chippies talk about the funnies in the papers.
> The cartoonists weep in their beer.
> Ship riveters talk with their feet
> To the feet of floozies under the tables.
A quartet of white hopes mourn with interspersed
> snickers:
>> "I got the blues.
>> I got the blues.
>> I got the blues."
And . . . as we said earlier:
> The cartoonists weep in their beer.

CRAPSHOOTERS

SOMEBODY loses whenever somebody wins.
This was known to the Chaldeans long ago.
And more: somebody wins whenever somebody loses.
This too was in the savvy of the Chaldeans.

They take it heaven's hereafter is an eternity of crap
    games where they try their wrists years and years
    and no police come with a wagon; the game goes
    on forever.
The spots on the dice are the music signs of the songs
    of heaven here.
God is Luck: Luck is God: we are all bones the
    High Thrower rolled: some are two spots, some
    double sixes.

The myths are Phoebe, Little Joe, Big Dick.
Hope runs high with a: Huh, seven—huh, come seven
This too was in the savvy of the Chaldeans.

SOUP

I saw a famous man eating soup.
I say he was lifting a fat broth
Into his mouth with a spoon.
His name was in the newspapers that day
Spelled out in tall black headlines
And thousands of people were talking about him.

    When I saw him,
He sat bending his head over a plate
Putting soup in his mouth with a spoon.

CLINTON SOUTH OF POLK

I WANDER down on Clinton street south of Polk
And listen to the voices of Italian children quarreling.
It is a cataract of coloratura
And I could sleep to their musical threats and accusa-
    tions.

BLUE ISLAND INTERSECTION

Six street ends come together here.
They feed people and wagons into the center.
In and out all day horses with thoughts of nose-bags,
Men with shovels, women with baskets and baby
  buggies.
Six ends of streets and no sleep for them all day.
The people and wagons come and go, out and in.
Triangles of banks and drug stores watch.
The policemen whistle, the trolley cars bump:
Wheels, wheels, feet, feet, all day.

In the false dawn when the chickens blink
And the east shakes a lazy baby toe at to-morrow,
And the east fixes a pink half-eye this way,
In the time when only one milk wagon crosses
These three streets, these six street ends,
It is the sleep time and they rest.
The triangle banks and drug stores rest.
The policeman is gone, his star and gun sleep.
The owl car blutters along in a sleep-walk.

RED-HEADED RESTAURANT CASHIER

SHAKE back your hair, O red-headed girl.
Let go your laughter and keep your two proud freckles
　　on your chin.
Somewhere is a man looking for a red-headed girl and
　　some day maybe he will look into your eyes for a
　　restaurant cashier and find a lover, maybe.
Around and around go ten thousand men hunting a
　　red headed girl with two freckles on her chin.
I have seen them hunting, hunting.
　　　　　Shake back your hair; let go your laughter.

BOY AND FATHER

THE boy Alexander understands his father to be a
famous lawyer.
The leather law books of Alexander's father fill a
room like hay in a barn.
Alexander has asked his father to let him build a house
like bricklayers build, a house with walls and
roofs made of big leather law books.

The rain beats on the windows
And the raindrops run down the window glass
And the raindrops slide off the green blinds
down the siding.
The boy Alexander dreams of Napoleon in John C.
Abbott's history, Napoleon the grand and lonely
man wronged, Napoleon in his life wronged and
in his memory wronged.
The boy Alexander dreams of the cat Alice saw, the
cat fading off into the dark and leaving the teeth
of its Cheshire smile lighting the gloom.

Buffaloes, blizzards, way down in Texas, in the pan-
handle of Texas snuggling close to New Mexico,
These creep into Alexander's dreaming by the window
when his father talks with strange men about
land down in Deaf Smith County.

Alexander's father tells the strange men: Five years ago we ran a Ford out on the prairie and chased antelopes.

Only once or twice in a long while has Alexander heard his father say "my first wife" so-and-so and such-and-such.

A few times softly the father has told Alexander, "Your mother . . . was a beautiful woman . . . but we won't talk about her."

Always Alexander listens with a keen listen when he hears his father mention "my first wife" or "Alexander's mother."

Alexander's father smokes a cigar and the Episcopal rector smokes a cigar and the words come often: mystery of life, mystery of life.

These two come into Alexander's head blurry and gray while the rain beats on the windows and the raindrops run down the window glass and the raindrops slide off the green blinds and down the siding.

These and: There is a God, there must be a God, how can there be rain or sun unless there is a God?

So from the wrongs of Napoleon and the Cheshire cat smile on to the buffaloes and blizzards of Texas and on to his mother and to God, so the blurry gray rain dreams of Alexander have gone on five minutes, maybe ten, keeping slow easy time to the raindrops on the window glass and the raindrops sliding off the green blinds and down the siding.

CLEAN CURTAINS

New neighbors came to the corner house at Congress and Green streets.

The look of their clean white curtains was the same as the rim of a nun's bonnet.

One way was an oyster pail factory, one way they made candy, one way paper boxes, strawboard cartons.

The warehouse trucks shook the dust of the ways loose and the wheels whirled dust—there was dust of hoof and wagon wheel and rubber tire— dust of police and fire wagons—dust of the winds that circled at midnights and noon listening to no prayers.

"O mother, I know the heart of you," I sang passing the rim of a nun's bonnet—O white curtains—and people clean as the prayers of Jesus here in the faded ramshackle at Congress and Green.

Dust and the thundering trucks won—the barrages of the street wheels and the lawless wind took their way—was it five weeks or six the little mother, the new neighbors, battled and then took away the white prayers in the windows?

CRIMSON CHANGES PEOPLE

DID I see a crucifix in your eyes
and nails and Roman soldiers
and a dusk Golgotha?

Did I see Mary, the changed woman,
washing the feet of all men,
clean as new grass
when the old grass burns?

Did I see moths in your eyes, lost moths,
with a flutter of wings that meant:
we can never come again.

Did I see No Man's Land in your eyes
and men with lost faces, lost loves,
and you among the stubs crying?

Did I see you in the red death jazz of war
losing moths among lost faces,
speaking to the stubs who asked you
to speak of songs and God and dancing,
of bananas, northern lights or Jesus,
any hummingbird of thought whatever
flying away from the red death jazz of war?

Did I see your hand make a useless gesture
trying to say with a code of five fingers
something the tongue only stutters?
did I see a dusk Golgotha?

NEIGHBORS

On Forty First Street
near Eighth Avenue
a frame house wobbles.

If houses went on crutches
this house would be
one of the cripples.

A sign on the house:
Church of the Living God
And Rescue Home for Orphan Children.

From a Greek coffee house
Across the street
A cabalistic jargon
Jabbers back.
    And men at tables
    Spill Peloponnesian syllables
    And speak of shovels for street work.
    And the new embankments of the Erie Railroad
    At Painted Post, Horse's Head, Salamanca.

CAHOOTS

PLAY it across the table.
What if we steal this city blind?
If they want any thing let 'em nail it down.

Harness bulls, dicks, front office men,
And the high goats up on the bench,
Ain't they all in cahoots?
Ain't it fifty-fifty all down the line,
Petemen, dips, boosters, stick-ups and guns—
        what's to hinder?

        Go fifty-fifty.
If they nail you call in a mouthpiece.
Fix it, you gazump, you slant-head, fix it.
        Feed 'em. . . .

Nothin' ever sticks to my fingers, nah, nah,
        nothin' like that,
But there ain't no law we got to wear mittens—
        huh—is there?
Mittens, that's a good one—mittens!
There oughta be a law everybody wear mittens.

BLUE MAROONS

"You slut," he flung at her.
It was more than a hundred times
He had thrown it into her face
And by this time it meant nothing to her.
She said to herself upstairs sweeping,
" Clocks are to tell time with, pitchers
Hold milk, spoons dip out gravy, and a
Coffee pot keeps the respect of those
Who drink coffee—I am a woman whose
Husband gives her a kiss once for ten
Times he throws it in my face, ' You slut.'
If I go to a small town and him along
Or if I go to a big city and him along,
What of it? Am I better off? " She swept
The upstairs and came downstairs to fix
Dinner for the family.

THE HANGMAN AT HOME

WHAT does the hangman think about
When he goes home at night from work?
When he sits down with his wife and
Children for a cup of coffee and a
Plate of ham and eggs, do they ask
Him if it was a good day's work
And everything went well or do they
Stay off some topics and talk about
The weather, base ball, politics
And the comic strips in the papers
And the movies? Do they look at his
Hands when he reaches for the coffee
Or the ham and eggs? If the little
Ones say, Daddy, play horse, here's
A rope—does he answer like a joke:
I seen enough rope for today?
Or does his face light up like a
Bonfire of joy and does he say:
It's a good and dandy world we live
In. And if a white face moon looks
In through a window where a baby girl
Sleeps and the moon gleams mix with
Baby ears and baby hair—the hangman—
How does he act then? It must be easy
For him. Anything is easy for a hangman,
I guess.

MAN, THE MAN-HUNTER

I SAW Man, the man-hunter,
Hunting with a torch in one hand
And a kerosene can in the other,
Hunting with guns, ropes, shackles.

I listened
And the high cry rang,
The high cry of Man, the man-hunter:
We'll get you yet,   you   sbxyzch!

I listened later.
The high cry rang:
Kill him!   kill him!   the sbxyzch!

In the morning the sun saw
Two butts of something, a smoking rump,
And a warning in charred wood:
                    Well, we got him,
                    the   sbxyzch.

THE SINS OF KALAMAZOO

THE sins of Kalamazoo are neither scarlet nor crimson.
The sins of Kalamazoo are a convict gray, a dishwater
drab.
And the people who sin the sins of Kalamazoo are
neither scarlet nor crimson.
They run to drabs and grays—and some of them sing
they shall be washed whiter than snow—and
some: We should worry.

Yes, Kalamazoo is a spot on the map
And the passenger trains stop there
And the factory smokestacks smoke
And the grocery stores are open Saturday nights
And the streets are free for citizens who vote
And inhabitants counted in the census.
Saturday night is the big night.
Listen with your ears on a Saturday night in
Kalamazoo
And say to yourself: I hear America, I hear,
what do I hear?

Main street there runs through the middle of the town
And there is a dirty postoffice
And a dirty city hall
And a dirty railroad station

And the United States flag cries, cries the Stars and
    Stripes to the four winds on Lincoln's birthday
    and the Fourth of July.

Kalamazoo kisses a hand to something far off.
Kalamazoo calls to a long horizon, to a shivering silver
    angel, to a creeping mystic what-is-it.
" We're here because we're here," is the song of Kala-
    mazoo.
" We don't know where we're going but we're on our
    way," are the words.
There are hound dogs of bronze on the public square,
    hound dogs looking far beyond the public square.

Sweethearts there in Kalamazoo
Go to the general delivery window of the postoffice
And speak their names and ask for letters
And ask again, " Are you sure there is nothing for me?
I wish you'd look again—there must be a letter for
    me."

And sweethearts go to the city hall
And tell their names and say, " We want a license."
And they go to an installment house and buy a bed on
    time and a clock
And the children grow up asking each other, " What
    can we do to kill time? "
They grow up and go to the railroad station and buy
    tickets for Texas, Pennsylvania, Alaska.
" Kalamazoo is all right," they say. " But I want to
    see the world."

And when they have looked the world over they come
 back saying it is all like Kalamazoo.

The trains come in from the east and hoot for the
 crossings,
And buzz away to the peach country and Chicago to
 the west
Or they come from the west and shoot on to the Battle
 Creek breakfast bazaars
And the speedbug heavens of Detroit.

" I hear America, I hear, *what* do I hear? "
Said a loafer lagging along on the sidewalks of Kal-
 amazoo,
Lagging along and asking questions, reading signs.

Oh yes, there is a town named Kalamazoo,
A spot on the map where the trains hesitate.
I saw the sign of a five and ten cent store there
And the Standard Oil Company and the International
 Harvester
And a graveyard and a ball grounds
And a short order counter where a man can get a
 stack of wheats
And a pool hall where a rounder leered confidential
 like and said:
" Lookin' for a quiet game? "

The loafer lagged along and asked,
" Do you make guitars here?
Do you make boxes the singing wood winds ask to
 sleep in?

Do you rig up strings the singing wood winds sift over
    and sing low?"
The answer: "We manufacture musical instruments
    here."

Here I saw churches with steeples like hatpins,
Undertaking rooms with sample coffins in the show
    window
And signs everywhere satisfaction is guaranteed,
Shooting galleries where men kill imitation pigeons,
And there were doctors for the sick,
And lawyers for people waiting in jail,
And a dog catcher and a superintendent of streets,
And telephones, water-works, trolley cars,
And newspapers with a splatter of telegrams from
    sister cities of Kalamazoo the round world over.

And the loafer lagging along said:
Kalamazoo, you ain't in a class by yourself;
I seen you before in a lot of places.
If you are nuts America is nuts.
        And lagging along he said bitterly:
        Before I came to Kalamazoo I was silent.
        Now I am gabby, God help me, I am gabby.

Kalamazoo, both of us will do a fadeaway.
I will be carried out feet first
And time and the rain will chew you to dust
And the winds blow you away.
And an old, old mother will lay a green moss cover
    on my bones

And a green moss cover on the stones of your postoffice and city hall.

Best of all
I have loved your kiddies playing run-sheep-run
And cutting their initials on the ball ground fence.
They knew every time I fooled them who was fooled
and how.

Best of all
I have loved the red gold smoke of your sunsets;
I have loved a moon with a ring around it
Floating over your public square;
I have loved the white dawn frost of early winter
silver
And purple over your railroad tracks and lumber
yards.

The wishing heart of you I loved, Kalamazoo.
I sang bye-lo, bye-lo to your dreams.
I sang bye-lo to your hopes and songs.
I wished to God there were hound dogs of bronze on
your public square,
Hound dogs with bronze paws looking to a long
horizon with a shivering silver angel,
a creeping mystic what-is-it.

BROKEN-FACE GARGOYLES

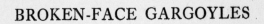

BROKEN-FACE GARGOYLES

ALL I can give you is broken-face gargoyles.
It is too early to sing and dance at funerals,
Though I can whisper to you I am looking for an
    undertaker humming a lullaby and throwing his
    feet in a swift and mystic buck-and-wing, now
    you see it and now you don't.

Fish to swim a pool in your garden flashing a speckled
    silver,
A basket of wine-saps filling your room with flame-
    dark for your eyes and the tang of valley orchards
    for your nose,
Such a beautiful pail of fish, such a beautiful peck
    of apples, I cannot bring you now.
It is too early and I am not footloose yet.

I shall come in the night when I come with a hammer
    and saw.
I shall come near your window, where you look out
    when your eyes open in the morning,
And there I shall slam together bird-houses and bird-
    baths for wing-loose wrens and hummers to live
    in, birds with yellow wing tips to blur and buzz
    soft all summer,

So I shall make little fool homes with doors, always open doors for all and each to run away when they want to.

I shall come just like that even though now it is early and I am not yet footloose,

Even though I am still looking for an undertaker with a raw, wind-bitten face and a dance in his feet.

I make a date with you (put it down) for six o'clock in the evening a thousand years from now.

All I can give you now is broken-face gargoyles.

All I can give you now is a double gorilla head with two fish mouths and four eagle eyes hooked on a street wall, spouting water and looking two ways to the ends of the street for the new people, the young strangers, coming, coming, always coming.

It is early.
I shall yet be footloose.

APRONS OF SILENCE

MANY things I might have said today.
And I kept my mouth shut.
So many times I was asked
To come and say the same things
Everybody was saying, no end
To the yes-yes, yes-yes,
      me-too, me-too.

The aprons of silence covered me.
A wire and hatch held my tongue.
I spit nails into an abyss and listened.
I shut off the gabble of Jones, Johnson, Smith,
All whose names take pages in the city directory.

I fixed up a padded cell and lugged it around.
I locked myself in and nobody knew it.
Only the keeper and the kept in the hoosegow
Knew it—on the streets, in the postoffice,
On the cars, into the railroad station
Where the caller was calling, " All a-board,
All a-board for . . Blaa-blaa . . Blaa-blaa,
Blaa-blaa . . and all points northwest . . all a-board."
Here I took along my own hoosegow
And did business with my own thoughts.
Do you see? It must be the aprons of silence.

DEATH SNIPS PROUD MEN

DEATH is stronger than all the governments because
the governments are men and men die and then
death laughs: Now you see 'em, now you don't.

Death is stronger than all proud men and so death
snips proud men on the nose, throws a pair of
dice and says: Read 'em and weep.

Death sends a radiogram every day: When I want
you I'll drop in—and then one day he comes with a
master-key and lets himself in and says: We'll
go now.

Death is a nurse mother with big arms: 'Twon't hurt
you at all; it's your time now; you just need a
long sleep, child; what have you had anyhow
better than sleep?

GOOD NIGHT

MANY ways to spell good night.

Fireworks at a pier on the Fourth of July
    spell it with red wheels and yellow spokes.
They fizz in the air, touch the water and quit.
Rockets make a trajectory of gold-and-blue
    and then go out.

Railroad trains at night spell with a smokestack
    mushrooming a white pillar.

Steamboats turn a curve in the Mississippi crying
    in a baritone that crosses lowland cottonfields
    to a razorback hill.

It is easy to spell good night.
                    Many ways to spell good night.

SHIRT

My shirt is a token and symbol,
more than a cover for sun and rain,
my shirt is a signal,
and a teller of souls.

I can take off my shirt and tear it,
and so make a ripping razzly noise,
and the people will say,
" Look at him tear his shirt."

I can keep my shirt on.
I can stick around and sing like a little bird
and look 'em all in the eye and never be fazed.
I can keep my shirt on.

JAZZ FANTASIA

DRUM on your drums, batter on your banjoes,
sob on the long cool winding saxophones.
Go to it, O jazzmen.

Sling your knuckles on the bottoms of the happy
tin pans, let your trombones ooze, and go husha-
husha-hush with the slippery sand-paper.

Moan like an autumn wind high in the lonesome tree-
tops, moan soft like you wanted somebody terrible,
cry like a racing car slipping away from a motorcycle
cop, bang-bang! you jazzmen, bang altogether drums,
traps, banjoes, horns, tin cans—make two people fight
on the top of a stairway and scratch each other's eyes
in a clinch tumbling down the stairs.

Can the rough stuff . . . now a Mississippi steamboat
pushes up the night river with a hoo-hoo-hoo-oo . . .
and the green lanterns calling to the high soft stars
. . . a red moon rides on the humps of the low river
hills . . . go to it, O jazzmen.

DO YOU WANT AFFIDAVITS?

THERE'S a hole in the bottom of the sea.
> Do you want affidavits?
There's a man in the moon with money for you.
> Do you want affidavits?
There are ten dancing girls in a sea-chamber off Nantucket waiting for you.
There are tall candles in Timbuctoo burning penance for you.
There are—anything else?
Speak now—for now we stand amid the great wishing windows—and the law says we are free to be wishing all this week at the windows.
Shall I raise my right hand and swear to you in the monotone of a notary public? this is "the truth, the whole truth, and nothing but the truth."

"OLD-FASHIONED REQUITED LOVE"

I HAVE ransacked the encyclopedias
And slid my fingers among topics and titles
Looking for you.

And the answer comes slow.
There seems to be no answer.

I shall ask the next banana peddler the who and the
    why of it.

Or—the iceman with his iron tongs gripping a clear
    cube in summer sunlight—maybe he will know.

PURPLE MARTINS

If we were such and so, the same as these,
maybe we too would be slingers and sliders,
tumbling half over in the water mirrors,
tumbling half over at the horse heads of the sun,
tumbling our purple numbers.

Twirl on, you and your satin blue.
Be water birds, be air birds.
Be these purple tumblers you are.

    Dip and get away
From loops into slip-knots,
Write your own ciphers and figure eights.
It is your wooded island here in Lincoln park.
Everybody knows this belongs to you.

    Five fat geese
Eat grass on a sod bank
And never count your slinging ciphers,
               your sliding figure eights,

A man on a green paint iron bench,
Slouches his feet and sniffs in a book,
And looks at you and your loops and slip-knots,
And looks at you and your sheaths of satin blue,
And slouches again and sniffs in the book,
And mumbles: It is an idle and a doctrinaire exploit.

Go on tumbling half over in the water mirrors.
Go on tumbling half over at the horse heads of the sun.
Be water birds, be air birds.
Be these purple tumblers you are.

BRASS KEYS

Joy . . . weaving two violet petals for a coat lapel . . .
painting on a slab of night sky a Christ face . . .
slipping new brass keys into rusty iron locks and
shouldering till at last the door gives and we are in
a new room . . . forever and ever violet petals, slabs,
the Christ face, brass keys and new rooms.

are we near or far? . . . is there anything else? . . .
who comes back? . . . and why does love ask nothing
and give all? and why is love rare as a tailed comet
shaking guesses out of men at telescopes ten feet long?
why does the mystery sit with its chin on the lean
forearm of women in gray eyes and women in hazel
eyes?

are any of these less proud, less important, than a
cross-examining lawyer? are any of these less perfect
than the front page of a morning newspaper?

the answers are not computed and attested in the back
of an arithmetic for the verifications of the lazy

there is no authority in the phone book for us to call
and ask the why, the wherefore, and the howbeit
it's . . . a riddle . . . by God

PICK-OFFS

THE telescope picks off star dust
on the clean steel sky and sends it to me.

The telephone picks off my voice and
sends it cross country a thousand miles.

The eyes in my head pick off pages of
Napoleon memoirs . . . a rag handler,
a head of dreams walks in a sheet of
mist . . . the palace panels shut in no-
bodies drinking nothings out of silver
helmets . . . in the end we all come to a
rock island and the hold of the sea-walls.

MANUFACTURED GODS

THEY put up big wooden gods.
Then they burned the big wooden gods
And put up brass gods and
Changing their minds suddenly
Knocked down the brass gods and put up
A doughface god with gold earrings.
The poor mutts, the pathetic slant heads,
They didn't know a little tin god
Is as good as anything in the line of gods
Nor how a little tin god answers prayer
And makes rain and brings luck
The same as a big wooden god or a brass
God or a doughface god with golden
Earrings.

MASK

To have your face left overnight
Flung on a board by a crazy sculptor;
To have your face drop off a board
And fall to pieces on a floor
Lost among lumps all finger-marked
          —How now?

To be calm and level, placed high,
Looking among perfect women bathing
And among bareheaded long-armed men,
Corner dreams of a crazy sculptor,
And then to fall, drop clean off the board,
Four o'clock in the morning and not a dog
Nor a policeman anywhere—

          Hoo hoo!
     had it been my laughing face
     maybe I would laugh with you,
     but my lover's face, the face I give
     women and the moon and the sea!

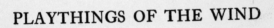

PLAYTHINGS OF THE WIND

FOUR PRELUDES ON PLAYTHINGS OF THE WIND

" The past is a bucket of ashes."

1

THE woman named To-morrow
sits with a hairpin in her teeth
and takes her time
and does her hair the way she wants it
and fastens at last the last braid and coil
and puts the hairpin where it belongs
and turns and drawls: Well, what of it?
My grandmother, Yesterday, is gone.
What of it? Let the dead be dead.

2

The doors were cedar
and the panels strips of gold
and the girls were golden girls
and the panels read and the girls chanted:
    We are the greatest city,
    the greatest nation:
    nothing like us ever was.

The doors are twisted on broken hinges.
Sheets of rain swish through on the wind
     where the golden girls ran and the panels
      read:
     We are the greatest city,
     the greatest nation,
     nothing like us ever was.

3

It has happened before.
Strong men put up a city and got
     a nation together,
And paid singers to sing and women
     to warble: We are the greatest city,
      the greatest nation,
      nothing like us ever was.

And while the singers sang
and the strong men listened
and paid the singers well
and felt good about it all,
    there were rats and lizards who listened
    . . . and the only listeners left now
    . . . are . . . the rats . . . and the lizards.

And there are black crows
crying, "Caw, caw,"
bringing mud and sticks
building a nest

over the words carved
on the doors where the panels were cedar
and the strips on the panels were gold
and the golden girls came singing:
    We are the greatest city,
    the greatest nation:
    nothing like us ever was.

The only singers now are crows crying, "Caw, caw,"
And the sheets of rain whine in the wind and doorways.
And the only listeners now are . . . the rats . . . and
    the lizards.

4

The feet of the rats
scribble on the door sills;
the hieroglyphs of the rat footprints
chatter the pedigrees of the rats
and babble of the blood
and gabble of the breed
of the grandfathers and the great-grandfathers
of the rats.

And the wind shifts
and the dust on a door sill shifts
and even the writing of the rat footprints
tells us nothing, nothing at all
about the greatest city, the greatest nation
where the strong men listened
and the women warbled: Nothing like us ever
    was.

BROKEN TABERNACLES

HAVE I broken the smaller tabernacles, O Lord?
And in the destruction of these set up the greater and
massive, the everlasting tabernacles?
I know nothing today, what I have done and why,
O Lord, only I have broken and broken tabernacles.
They were beautiful in a way, these tabernacles torn
down by strong hands swearing—
They were beautiful—why did the hypocrites carve
their own names on the corner-stones? why did
the hypocrites keep on singing their own names
in their long noses every Sunday in these tabernacles?
Who lays any blame here among the split corner-
stones?

OSSAWATOMIE

I DON'T know how he came,
shambling, dark, and strong.

He stood in the city and told men:
My people are fools, my people are young and strong,
    my people must learn, my people are terrible
    workers and fighters.
Always he kept on asking: Where did that blood come
  from?

  They said: You for the fool killer,
         you for the booby hatch
         and a necktie party.

  They hauled him into jail.
  They sneered at him and spit on him,
  And he wrecked their jails,
  Singing, "God damn your jails,"
  And when he was most in jail
  Crummy among the crazy in the dark
  Then he was most of all out of jail
  Shambling, dark, and strong,
Always asking: Where did that blood come from?

They laid hands on him
And the fool killers had a laugh
And the necktie party was a go, by God.
They laid hands on him and he was a goner.
They hammered him to pieces and he stood up.
They buried him and he walked out of the grave, by God,
Asking again: Where did that blood come from?

LONG GUNS

THEN came, Oscar, the time of the guns.
And there was no land for a man, no land for a
    country,
       Unless guns sprang up
       And spoke their language.
The how of running the world was all in guns.

The law of a God keeping sea and land apart,
The law of a child sucking milk,
The law of stars held together,
       They slept and worked in the heads of men
       Making twenty mile guns, sixty mile guns,
       Speaking their language
       Of no land for a man, no land for a country
Unless . . . guns . . . unless . . . guns.

There was a child wanted the moon shot off the sky,
       asking a long gun to get the moon,
       to conquer the insults of the moon,
       to conquer something, anything,
       to put it over and win the day,
To show them the running of the world was all in guns.
There was a child wanted the moon shot off the sky.
They dreamed . . . in the time of the guns . . . of guns.

DUSTY DOORS

CHILD of the Aztec gods,
how long must we listen here,
how long before we go?

The dust is deep on the lintels.
The dust is dark on the doors.
If the dreams shake our bones,
    what can we say or do?

Since early morning we waited.
Since early, early morning, child.
There must be dreams on the way now.
There must be a song for our bones.

The dust gets deeper and darker.
Do the doors and lintels shudder?
    How long must we listen here?
    How long before we go?

FLASH CRIMSON

I SHALL cry God to give me a broken foot.

I shall ask for a scar and a slashed nose.

I shall take the last and the worst.

I shall be eaten by gray creepers in a bunkhouse where no runners of the sun come and no dogs live.

And yet—of all " and yets " this is the bronze strongest—

I shall keep one thing better than all else; there is the blue steel of a great star of early evening in it; it lives longer than a broken foot or any scar.

The broken foot goes to a hole dug with a shovel or the bone of a nose may whiten on a hilltop—and yet—" and yet "—

There is one crimson pinch of ashes left after all; and none of the shifting winds that whip the grass and none of the pounding rains that beat the dust, know how to touch or find the flash of this crimson.

I cry God to give me a broken foot, a scar, or a lousy
death.

I who have seen the flash of this crimson, I ask God
for the last and worst.

THE LAWYERS KNOW TOO MUCH

THE lawyers, Bob, know too much.
They are chums of the books of old John Marshall.
They know it all, what a dead hand wrote,
A stiff dead hand and its knuckles crumbling,
The bones of the fingers a thin white ash.
    The lawyers know
    a dead man's thoughts too well.

In the heels of the higgling lawyers, Bob,
Too many slippery ifs and buts and howevers,
Too much hereinbefore provided whereas,
Too many doors to go in and out of.

    When the lawyers are through
    What is there left, Bob?
    Can a mouse nibble at it
    And find enough to fasten a tooth in?

    Why is there always a secret singing
    When a lawyer cashes in?
    Why does a hearse horse snicker
    Hauling a lawyer away?

The work of a bricklayer goes to the blue.
The knack of a mason outlasts a moon.
The hands of a plasterer hold a room together.
The land of a farmer wishes him back again.
    Singers of songs and dreamers of plays
    Build a house no wind blows over.
The lawyers—tell me why a hearse horse snickers
    hauling a lawyer's bones.

LOSERS

If I should pass the tomb of Jonah
I would stop there and sit for awhile;
Because I was swallowed one time deep in the dark
And came out alive after all.

If I pass the burial spot of Nero
I shall say to the wind, "Well, well!"—
I who have fiddled in a world on fire,
I who have done so many stunts not worth doing.

I am looking for the grave of Sinbad too.
I want to shake his ghost-hand and say,
"Neither of us died very early, did we?"

And the last sleeping-place of Nebuchadnezzar—
When I arrive there I shall tell the wind:
"You ate grass; I have eaten crow—
Who is better off now or next year?"

Jack Cade, John Brown, Jesse James,
There too I could sit down and stop for awhile.
I think I could tell their headstones:
"God, let me remember all good losers."

I could ask people to throw ashes on their heads
In the name of that sergeant at Belleau Woods,
Walking into the drumfires, calling his men,
"Come on, you . . . Do you want to live forever?"

PLACES

Roses and gold
For you today,
And the flash of flying flags.

I will have
Ashes,
Dust in my hair,
Crushes of hoofs.

Your name
Fills the mouth
Of rich man and poor.
Women bring
Armfuls of flowers
And throw on you.

I go hungry
Down in dreams
And loneliness,
Across the rain
To slashed hills
Where men wait and hope for me.

THREES

I was a boy when I heard three red words
a thousand Frenchmen died in the streets
for: Liberty, Equality, Fraternity—I asked
why men die for words.

I was older; men with mustaches, sideburns,
lilacs, told me the high golden words are:
Mother, Home, and Heaven—other older men with
face decorations said: God, Duty, Immortality
—they sang these threes slow from deep lungs.

Years ticked off their say-so on the great clocks
of doom and damnation, soup and nuts: meteors flashed
their say-so: and out of great Russia came three
dusky syllables workmen took guns and went out to die
for: Bread, Peace, Land.

And I met a marine of the U. S. A., a leatherneck with
a girl on his knee for a memory in ports circling the
earth and he said: Tell me how to say three things
and I always get by—gimme a plate of ham and eggs—
how much?—and—do you love me, kid?

THE LIARS
(*March, 1919*)

A LIAR goes in fine clothes.
A liar goes in rags.
A liar is a liar, clothes or no clothes.
A liar is a liar and lives on the lies he tells
            and dies in a life of lies.
And the stonecutters earn a living—with lies—
            on the tombs of liars.

A liar looks 'em in the eye
And lies to a woman,
Lies to a man, a pal, a child, a fool.
And he is an old liar; we know him many years back.

  A liar lies to nations.
  A liar lies to the people.
A liar takes the blood of the people
And drinks this blood with a laugh and a lie,
  A laugh in his neck,
  A lie in his mouth.
And this liar is an old one; we know him many years.
  He is straight as a dog's hind leg.
  He is straight as a corkscrew.
He is white as a black cat's foot at midnight.

The tongue of a man is tied on this,
On the liar who lies to nations,
The liar who lies to the people.
The tongue of a man is tied on this
And ends: To hell with 'em all.
   To hell with 'em all.

It's a song hard as a riveter's hammer,
 Hard as the sleep of a crummy hobo,
 Hard as the sleep of a lousy doughboy,
Twisted as a shell-shock idiot's gibber.

The liars met where the doors were locked.
They said to each other: Now for war.
The liars fixed it and told 'em: Go.

Across their tables they fixed it up,
Behind their doors away from the mob.
And the guns did a job that nicked off millions.
The guns blew seven million off the map,
The guns sent seven million west.
Seven million shoving up the daisies.
Across their tables they fixed it up,
   The liars who lie to nations.

 And now
 Out of the butcher's job
 And the boneyard junk the maggots have cleaned,
 Where the jaws of skulls tell the jokes of war ghosts,
Out of this they are calling now: Let's go back where
  we were.
   Let us run the world again, us, us.

Where the doors are locked the liars say: Wait and
    we'll cash in again.

So I hear The People talk.
I hear them tell each other:
    Let the strong men be ready.
    Let the strong men watch.
    Let your wrists be cool and your head clear.
    Let the liars get their finish,
    The liars and their waiting game, waiting a day again
    To open the doors and tell us: War! get out to your
        war again.

So I hear The People tell each other:
    Look at to-day and to-morrow.
    Fix this clock that nicks off millions
    When The Liars say it's time.
    Take things in your own hands.
            To hell with 'em all,
    The liars who lie to nations,
    The liars who lie to The People.

PRAYER AFTER WORLD WAR

Wandering oversea dreamer,
Hunting and hoarse, Oh daughter and mother,
Oh daughter of ashes and mother of blood,
Child of the hair let down, and tears,
Child of the cross in the south
And the star in the north,
Keeper of Egypt and Russia and France,
Keeper of England and Poland and Spain,
Make us a song for to-morrow.
Make us one new dream, us who forget,
Out of the storm let us have one star.

Struggle, Oh anvils, and help her.
Weave with your wool, Oh winds and skies.
Let your iron and copper help,
        Oh dirt of the old dark earth.

Wandering oversea singer,
Singing of ashes and blood,
Child of the scars of fire,
    Make us one new dream, us who forget.
    Out of the storm let us have one star.

A. E. F.

THERE will be a rusty gun on the wall, sweetheart,
The rifle grooves curling with flakes of rust.
A spider will make a silver string nest in the
      darkest, warmest corner of it.
The trigger and the range-finder, they too will be rusty.
And no hands will polish the gun, and it will hang
    on the wall.
Forefingers and thumbs will point absently and casu-
    ally toward it.
It will be spoken among half-forgotten, wished-to-be-
    forgotten things.
They will tell the spider: Go on, you're doing good
    work.

BAS-RELIEF

Five geese deploy mysteriously.
Onward proudly with flagstaffs,
Hearses with silver bugles,
Bushels of plum-blossoms dropping
For ten mystic web-feet—
Each his own drum-major,
Each charged with the honor
Of the ancient goose nation,
Each with a nose-length surpassing
The nose-lengths of rival nations.
Somberly, slowly, unimpeachably,
Five geese deploy mysteriously.

CARLOVINGIAN DREAMS

COUNT these reminiscences like money.
The Greeks had their picnics under another name.
The Romans wore glad rags and told their neighbors,
    "What of it?"
The Carlovingians hauling logs on carts, they too
Stuck their noses in the air and stuck their thumbs to
    their noses
And tasted life as a symphonic dream of fresh eggs
    broken over a frying pan left by an uncle who
    killed men with spears and short swords.
Count these reminiscences like money.

        Drift, and drift on, white ships.
Sailing the free sky blue, sailing and changing and
    sailing,
Oh, I remember in the blood of my dreams how they
    sang before me.
Oh, they were men and women who got money for
    their work, money or love or dreams.
            Sail on, white ships.
            Let me have spring dreams.
Let me count reminiscences like money; let me count
    picnics, glad rags and the great bad manners of
    the Carlovingians breaking fresh eggs in the cop-
    per pans of their proud uncles.

BRONZES

THEY ask me to handle bronzes
Kept by children in China
Three thousand years
Since their fathers
Took fire and molds and hammers
And made these.

The Ming, the Chou,
And other dynasties,
Out, gone, reckoned in ciphers,
Dynasties dressed up
In old gold and old yellow—
They saw these.

Let the wheels
Of three thousand years
Turn, turn, turn on.

Let one poet then
(One will be enough)
Handle these bronzes
And mention the dynasties
And pass them along.

LET LOVE GO ON

Let it go on; let the love of this hour be poured out
till all the answers are made, the last dollar spent
and the last blood gone.

Time runs with an ax and a hammer, time slides down
the hallways with a pass-key and a master-key,
and time gets by, time wins.

Let the love of this hour go on; let all the oaths and
children and people of this love be clean as a
washed stone under a waterfall in the sun.

Time is a young man with ballplayer legs, time runs
a winning race against life and the clocks, time
tickles with rust and spots.

Let love go on; the heartbeats are measured out with
a measuring glass, so many apiece to gamble with,
to use and spend and reckon; let love go on.

KILLERS

I AM put high over all others in the city today.
I am the killer who kills for those who wish a killing
today.

Here is a strong young man who killed.
There was a driving wind of city dust and horse dung
blowing and he stood at an intersection of five
sewers and there pumped the bullets of an auto-
matic pistol into another man, a fellow citizen.
Therefore, the prosecuting attorneys, fellow citizens,
and a jury of his peers, also fellow citizens, listened to the testimony of other fellow citizens,
policemen, doctors, and after a verdict of guilty,
the judge, a fellow citizen, said: I sentence you
to be hanged by the neck till you are dead.

So there is a killer to be killed and I am the killer of
the killer for today.
I don't know why it beats in my head in the lines I
read once in an old school reader: I'm to be queen
of the May, mother, I'm to be queen of the May.
Anyhow it comes back in language just like that today.

I am the high honorable killer today.
There are five million people in the state, five million
killers for whom I kill
I am the killer who kills today for five million killers
who wish a killing.

CLEAN HANDS

IT is something to face the sun and know you are free.
To hold your head in the shafts of daylight slanting
the earth
And know your heart has kept a promise and the blood
runs clean:
It is something.
To go one day of your life among all men with clean
hands,
Clean for the day book today and the record of the
after days,
Held at your side proud, satisfied to the last, and ready,
So to have clean hands:
God, it is something,
One day of life so
And a memory fastened till the stars sputter out
And a love washed as white linen in the noon
drying.
Yes, go find the men of clean hands one day and see
the life, the memory, the love they have, to stay
longer than the plunging sea wets the shores or
the fires heave under the crust of the earth.
O yes, clean hands is the chant and only one man
knows its sob and its undersong and he dies
clenching the secret more to him than any woman
or chum.

And O the great brave men, the silent little brave
men, proud of their hands—clutching the knuckles
of their fingers into fists ready for death and the
dark, ready for life and the fight, the pay and the
memories—O the men proud of their hands.

THREE GHOSTS

THREE tailors of Tooley Street wrote: We, the People.
The names are forgotten. It is a joke in ghosts.

Cutters or bushelmen or armhole basters, they sat
cross-legged stitching, snatched at scissors, stole each
other thimbles.

Cross-legged, working for wages, joking each other
as misfits cut from the cloth of a Master Tailor,
they sat and spoke their thoughts of the glory of
The People, they met after work and drank beer to
The People.

Faded off into the twilights the names are forgotten.
It is a joke in ghosts. Let it ride. They wrote: We,
The People.

PENCILS

Pencils
telling where the wind comes from
open a story.

Pencils
telling where the wind goes
end a story.

These eager pencils
come to a stop
. . only . . when the stars high over
come to a stop.

Out of cabalistic to-morrows
come cryptic babies calling life
a strong and a lovely thing.

I have seen neither these
nor the stars high over
come to a stop.

Neither these nor the sea horses
running with the clocks of the moon.
Nor even a shooting star
snatching a pencil of fire
writing a curve of gold and white.

Like you . . I counted the shooting stars of a
winter night and my head was dizzy with all
of them calling one by one:

Look for us again.

JUG

THE shale and water thrown together so-so first of all,
Then a potter's hand on the wheel and his fingers shaping the jug; out of the mud a mouth and a handle;
Slimpsy, loose and ready to fall at a touch, fire plays on it, slow fire coaxing all the water out of the shale mix.
Dipped in glaze more fire plays on it till a molasses lava runs in waves, rises and retreats, a varnish of volcanoes.
Take it now; out of mud now here is a mouth and handle; out of this now mothers will pour milk and maple syrup and cider, vinegar, apple juice, and sorghum.
There is nothing proud about this; only one out of many; the potter's wheel slings them out and the fires harden them hours and hours thousands and thousands.
" Be good to me, put me down easy on the floors of the new concrete houses; I was poured out like a concrete house and baked in fire too."

AND THIS WILL BE ALL?

AND this will be all?
And the gates will never open again?
And the dust and the wind will play around the rusty
    door hinges and the songs of October moan, Why-
    oh, why-oh?

And you will look to the mountains
And the mountains will look to you
And you will wish you were a mountain
And the mountain will wish nothing at all?
       This will be all?
The gates will never-never open again?

The dust and the wind only
And the rusty door hinges and moaning October
And Why-oh, why-oh, in the moaning dry leaves,
       This will be all?

Nothing in the air but songs
And no singers, no mouths to know the songs?
You tell us a woman with a heartache tells you it is so?
       This will be all?

HOODLUMS

I AM a hoodlum, you are a hoodlum, we and all of us
are a world of hoodlums—maybe so.

I hate and kill better men than I am, so do you, so
do all of us—maybe—maybe so.

In the ends of my fingers the itch for another man's
neck, I want to see him hanging, one of dusk's
cartoons against the sunset.

This is the hate my father gave me, this was in my
mother's milk, this is you and me and all of us
in a world of hoodlums—maybe so.

Let us go on, brother hoodlums, let us kill and kill, it
has always been so, it will always be so, there is
nothing more to it.

Let us go on, sister hoodlums, kill, kill, and kill, the
torsoes of the world's mother's are tireless and the
loins of the world's fathers are strong—so go on
—kill, kill, kill.

Lay them deep in the dirt, the stiffs we fixed, the
cadavers bumped off, lay them deep and let the
night winds of winter blizzards howl their burial
service.

The night winds and the winter, the great white sheets
of northern blizzards, who can sing better for the
lost hoodlums the old requiem, " Kill him! kill
him! . . ."

Today my son, to-morrow yours, the day after your
next door neighbor's—it is all in the wrists of
the gods who shoot craps—it is anybody's guess
whose eyes shut next.

Being a hoodlum now, you and I, being all of us a
world of hoodlums, let us take up the cry when
the mob sluffs by on a thousand shoe soles, let
us too yammer, " Kill him! kill him! . . ."

Let us do this now . . . for our mothers . . . for our
sisters and wives . . . let us kill, kill, kill—for
the torsoes of the women are tireless and the
loins of the men are strong.

Chicago, July 29, 1919.

YES, THE DEAD SPEAK TO US

YES, the Dead speak to us.
This town belongs to the Dead, to the Dead and to
the Wilderness.

Back of the clamps on a fireproof door they hold the
papers of the Dead in a house here
And when two living men fall out, when one says the
Dead spoke a Yes, and the other says the Dead
spoke a No, they go then together to this house.

They loosen the clamps and haul at the hasps and try
their keys and curse at the locks and the combina-
tion numbers.
For the teeth of the rats are barred and the tongues
of the moths are outlawed and the sun and the
air of wind is not wanted.

They open a box where a sheet of paper shivers, in a
dusty corner shivers with the dry inkdrops of the
Dead, the signed names.
Here the ink testifies, here we find the say-so, here
we learn the layout, now we know where the
cities and farms belong.

Dead white men and dead red men
tested each other with shot and
knives; they twisted each others'
necks; land was yours if you took and
kept it.

How are the heads the rain seeps
in, the rain-washed knuckles in
sod and gumbo?

Where the sheets of paper shiver,
Back of the hasps and handles,
Back of the fireproof clamps,
They read what the fingers scribbled, who the land
belongs to now—it is herein provided, it is hereby
stipulated—the land and all appurtenances thereto and
all deposits of oil and gold and coal and silver, and
all pockets and repositories of gravel and diamonds,
dung and permanganese, and all clover and bumblebees,
all bluegrass, johnny-jump-ups, grassroots, springs of
running water or rivers or lakes or high spreading
trees or hazel bushes or sumach or thorn-apple branches
or high in the air the bird nest with spotted blue eggs
shaken in the roaming wind of the treetops—
    So it is scrawled here,
    " I direct and devise
    So and so and such and such,"
    And this is the last word,
    There is nothing more to it.

In a shanty out in the Wilderness, ghosts of to-morrow
sit, waiting to come and go, to do their job.

They will go into the house of the Dead and take the
shivering sheets of paper and make a bonfire and
dance a deadman's dance over the hissing crisp.

In a slang their own the dancers out of the Wilderness
will write a paper for the living to read and sign:

The dead need peace, the dead need sleep, let the dead
have peace and sleep, let the papers of the Dead
who fix the lives of the Living, let them be a
hissing crisp and ashes, let the young men and the
young women forever understand we are through
and no longer take the say-so of the Dead;

Let the dead have honor from us with our thoughts
of them and our thoughts of land and all appurtenances thereto and all deposits of oil and gold
and coal and silver, and all pockets and repositories
of gravel and diamonds, dung and permanganese,
and all clover and bumblebees, all bluegrass,
johnny-jump-ups, grassroots, springs of running
water or rivers or lakes or high spreading trees
or hazel bushes or sumach or thornapple branches
or high in the air the bird nest with spotted blue
eggs shaken in the roaming wind of the treetops.

And so, it is a shack of ghosts, a lean-to they have in
the Wilderness, and they are waiting and they
have learned strange songs how easy it is to wait
and how anything comes to those who wait long
enough and how most of all it is easy to wait for
death, and waiting, dream of new cities.

MIST FORMS

CALLS

BECAUSE I have called to you
as the flame flamingo calls,
or the want of a spotted hawk
is called—
            because in the dusk
the warblers shoot the running
waters of short songs to the
homecoming warblers—
                    because
the cry here is wing to wing
and song to song—

    I am waiting,
waiting with the flame flamingo,
the spotted hawk, the running water
warbler—
            waiting for you.

SEA-WASH

THE sea-wash never ends.
The sea-wash repeats, repeats.
Only old songs? Is that all the sea knows?
      Only the old strong songs?
      Is that all?
The sea-wash repeats, repeats.

SILVER WIND

Do you know how the dream looms? how if summer
misses one of us the two of us miss summer—

Summer when the lungs of the earth take a long
breath for the change to low contralto singing
mornings when the green corn leaves first break
through the black loam—

And another long breath for the silver soprano melody
of the moon songs in the light nights when the
earth is lighter than a feather, the iron mountains
lighter than a goose down—

So I shall look for you in the light nights then, in the
laughter of slats of silver under a hill hickory.

In the listening tops of the hickories, in the wind
motions of the hickory shingle leaves, in the imi-
tations of slow sea water on the shingle silver
in the wind—

     I shall look for you.

EVENING WATERFALL

WHAT was the name you called me? —
And why did you go so soon?

The crows lift their caw on the wind,
And the wind changed and was lonely.

The warblers cry their sleepy-songs
Across the valley gloaming,
Across the cattle-horns of early stars.

Feathers and people in the crotch of a treetop
Throw an evening waterfall of sleepy-songs.

What was the name you called me?—
And why did you go so soon?

CRUCIBLE

Hot gold runs a winding stream on the inside of a
    green bowl.

Yellow trickles in a fan figure, scatters a line of
    skirmishers, spreads a chorus of dancing girls,
    performs blazing ochre evolutions, gathers the
    whole show into one stream, forgets the past and
    rolls on.

The sea-mist green of the bowl's bottom is a dark
    throat of sky crossed by quarreling forks of
    umber and ochre and yellow changing faces.

SUMMER STARS

BEND low again, night of summer stars.
So near you are, sky of summer stars,
So near, a long arm man can pick off stars,
Pick off what he wants in the sky bowl,
So near you are, summer stars,
So near, strumming, strumming,
            So lazy and hum-strumming.

THROW ROSES

THROW roses on the sea where the dead went down.
  The roses speak to the sea,
  And the sea to the dead.
Throw roses, O lovers—
  Let the leaves wash on the salt in the sun.

JUST BEFORE APRIL CAME

The snow piles in dark places are gone.
Pools by the railroad tracks shine clear.
The gravel of all shallow places shines.
A white pigeon reels and somersaults.

Frogs plutter and squdge—and frogs beat
        the air with a recurring thin
        steel sliver of melody.
Crows go in fives and tens; they march their
        black feathers past a blue pool; they
        celebrate an old festival.
A spider is trying his webs, a pink bug sits
        on my hand washing his forelegs.
I might ask: Who are these people?

STARS, SONGS, FACES

GATHER the stars if you wish it so.
Gather the songs and keep them.
Gather the faces of women.
Gather for keeping years and years.
　　　　And then . . .
Loosen your hands, let go and say good-by.
　　Let the stars and songs go.
　　Let the faces and years go.
　　Loosen your hands and say good-by.

SANDPIPERS

TEN miles of flat land along the sea.
Sandland where the salt water kills the
 sweet potatoes.
Homes for sandpipers—the script of their
 feet is on the sea shingles—they write
 in the morning, it is gone at noon—they
 write at noon, it is gone at night.
Pity the land, the sea, the ten mile flats,
 pity anything but the sandpiper's wire
 legs and feet.

THREE VIOLINS

THREE violins are trying their hearts.
The piece is MacDowell's Wild Rose.
  And the time of the wild rose
  And the leaves of the wild rose
And the dew-shot eyes of the wild rose
Sing in the air over three violins.
Somebody like you was in the heart of MacDowell.
Somebody like you is in three violins.

THE WIND SINGS WELCOME IN EARLY SPRING

(*For Paula*)

THE grip of the ice is gone now.
The silvers chase purple.
The purples tag silver.
　　They let out their runners
Here where summer says to the lilies:
　　"Wish and be wistful,
Circle this wind-hunted, wind-sung water."

Come along always, come along now.
You for me, kiss me, pull me by the ear.
Push me along with the wind push.
Sing like the whinnying wind.
Sing like the hustling obstreperous wind.

Have you ever seen deeper purple . . .
　　this in my wild wind fingers?
Could you have more fun with a pony or a goat?
Have you seen such flicking heels before,
Silver jig heels on the purple sky rim?
　　Come along always, come along now.

TAWNY

THESE are the tawny days: your face comes back.

The grapes take on purple: the sunsets redden
early on the trellis.

The bashful mornings hurl gray mist on the stripes
of sunrise.

Creep, silver on the field, the frost is welcome.

Run on, yellow balls on the hills, and you tawny
pumpkin flowers, chasing your lines of orange.

Tawny days: and your face again.

SLIPPERY

THE six month child
Fresh from the tub
Wriggles in our hands.
This is our fish child.
Give her a nickname: Slippery.

HELGA

THE wishes on this child's mouth
Came like snow on marsh cranberries;
The tamarack kept something for her;
The wind is ready to help her shoes.
The north has loved her; she will be
A grandmother feeding geese on frosty
Mornings; she will understand
Early snow on the cranberries
Better and better then.

BABY TOES

THERE is a blue star, Janet,
Fifteen years' ride from us,
If we ride a hundred miles an hour.

There is a white star, Janet,
Forty years' ride from us,
If we ride a hundred miles an hour.

Shall we ride
To the blue star
Or the white star?

PEOPLE WITH PROUD CHINS

I TELL them where the wind comes from,
Where the music goes when the fiddle is in the box.

Kids—I saw one with a proud chin, a sleepyhead,
And the moonline creeping white on her pillow.
  I have seen their heads in the starlight
  And their proud chins marching in a mist of stars.

They are the only people I never lie to.
  I give them honest answers,
Answers shrewd as the circles of white on brown
    chestnuts.

WINTER MILK

THE milk drops on your chin, Helga,
Must not interfere with the cranberry red of your
    cheeks
Nor the sky winter blue of your eyes.
Let your mammy keep hands off the chin.
This is a high holy spatter of white on the reds and
    blues.

Before the bottle was taken away,
Before you so proudly began today
Drinking your milk from the rim of a cup
They did not splash this high holy white on your chin.

There are dreams in your eyes, Helga.
Tall reaches of wind sweep the clear blue.
The winter is young yet, so young.
Only a little cupful of winter has touched your lips.
Drink on . . . milk with your lips . . . dreams with
    your eyes.

SLEEPYHEADS

SLEEP is a maker of makers. Birds sleep. Feet cling to a perch. Look at the balance. Let the legs loosen, the backbone untwist, the head go heavy over, the whole works tumbles a done bird off the perch.

Fox cubs sleep. The pointed head curls round into hind legs and tail. It is a ball of red hair. It is a muff waiting. A wind might whisk it in the air across pastures and rivers, a cocoon, a pod of seeds. The snooze of the black nose is in a circle of red hair.

Old men sleep. In chimney corners, in rocking chairs, at wood stoves, steam radiators. They talk and forget and nod and are out of talk with closed eyes. Forgetting to live. Knowing the time has come useless for them to live. Old eagles and old dogs run and fly in the dreams.

Babies sleep. In flannels the papoose faces, the bambino noses, and dodo, dodo the song of many matushkas. Babies—a leaf on a tree in the spring sun. A nub of a new thing sucks the sap of a tree in the sun, yes a new thing, a what-is-it? A left hand stirs, an eyelid twitches, the milk in the belly bubbles and gets to be blood and a left hand and an eyelid. Sleep is a maker of makers.

SUMACH AND BIRDS

IF you never came with a pigeon rainbow purple
Shining in the six o'clock September dusk:
If the red sumach on the autumn roads
Never danced on the flame of your eyelashes:
If the red-haws never burst in a million
Crimson fingertwists of your heartcrying:
If all this beauty of yours never crushed me
Then there are many flying acres of birds for me,
Many drumming gray wings going home I shall see,
Many crying voices riding the north wind.

WOMEN WASHING THEIR HAIR

THEY have painted and sung
the women washing their hair,
and the plaits and strands in the sun,
and the golden combs
and the combs of elephant tusks
and the combs of buffalo horn and hoof.

The sun has been good to women,
drying their heads of hair
as they stooped and shook their shoulders
and framed their faces with copper
and framed their eyes with dusk or chestnut.

The rain has been good to women.
If the rain should forget,
if the rain left off for a year—
the heads of women would wither,
the copper, the dusk and chestnuts, go.

They have painted and sung
the women washing their hair—
reckon the sun and rain in, too.

PEACH BLOSSOMS

WHAT cry of peach blossoms
　　let loose on the air today
I heard with my face thrown
　　in the pink-white of it all?
　　in the red whisper of it all?

What man I heard saying:
　　Christ, these are beautiful!

And Christ and Christ was in his mouth,
　　over these peach blossoms?

HALF MOON IN A HIGH WIND

MONEY is nothing now, even if I had it,
O mooney moon, yellow half moon,
Up over the green pines and gray elms,
Up in the new blue.

Streel, streel,
White lacey mist sheets of cloud,
Streel in the blowing of the wind,
Streel over the blue-and-moon sky,
Yellow gold half moon. It is light
On the snow; it is dark on the snow,
Streel, O lacey thin sheets, up in the new blue.

Come down, stay there, move on.
I want you, I don't, keep all.
There is no song to your singing.
I am hit deep, you drive far,
O mooney yellow half moon,
Steady, steady; or will you tip over?
Or will the wind and the streeling
Thin sheets only pass and move on
And leave you alone and lovely?
I want you, I don't, come down,
Stay there, move on.
Money is nothing now, even if I had it.

REMORSE

THE horse's name was Remorse.
There were people said, " Gee, what a nag ! "
And they were Edgar Allan Poe bugs and so
They called him Remorse.
                              When he was a gelding
He flashed his heels to other ponies
And threw dust in the noses of other ponies
And won his first race and his second
And another and another and hardly ever
Came under the wire behind the other runners.

And so, Remorse, who is gone, was the hero of a play
By Henry Blossom, who is now gone.

What is there to a monicker ? Call me anything.
A nut, a cheese, something that the cat brought in.
    Nick me with any old name.
Class me up for a fish, a gorilla, a slant head, an egg,
        a ham.
Only . . . slam me across the ears sometimes . . .
        and hunt for a white star
In my forehead and twist the bang of my forelock
        around it.
Make a wish for me. Maybe I will light out like a
        streak of wind.

RIVER MOONS

The double moon, one on the high back drop of the
    west, one on the curve of the river face,
The sky moon of fire and the river moon of water,
    I am taking these home in a basket, hung on an
    elbow, such a teeny weeny elbow, in my head.
I saw them last night, a cradle moon, two horns of
    a moon, such an early hopeful moon, such a child's
    moon for all young hearts to make a picture of.
The river—I remember this like a picture—the river
    was the upper twist of a written question mark.
I know now it takes many many years to write a river,
    a twist of water asking a question.
And white stars moved when the moon moved, and
    one red star kept burning, and the Big Dipper was
    almost overhead.

SAND SCRIBBLINGS

THE wind stops, the wind begins.
The wind says stop, begin.

A sea shovel scrapes the sand floor.
The shovel changes, the floor changes.

The sandpipers, maybe they know.
Maybe a three-pointed foot can tell.
Maybe the fog moon they fly to, guesses.

The sandpipers cheep " Here " and get away.
Five of them fly and keep together flying.

Night hair of some sea woman
Curls on the sand when the sea leaves
The salt tide without a good-by.

Boxes on the beach are empty.
Shake 'em and the nails loosen.
They have been somewhere.

HOW YESTERDAY LOOKED

THE high horses of the sea broke their white riders
On the walls that held and counted the hours
The wind lasted.

Two landbirds looked on and the north and the east
Looked on and the wind poured cups of foam
And the evening began.

The old men in the shanties looked on and lit their
Pipes and the young men spoke of the girls
For a wild night like this.

The south and the west looked on and the moon came
When the wind went down and the sea was sorry
And the singing slow.

Ask how the sunset looked between the wind going
Down and the moon coming up and I would struggle
To tell the how of it.

I give you fire here, I give you water, I give you
The wind that blew them across and across,
The scooping, mixing wind.

PAULA

NOTHING else in this song—only your face.
Nothing else here—only your drinking, night-gray eyes.

The pier runs into the lake straight as a rifle barrel.
I stand on the pier and sing how I know you mornings.
It is not your eyes, your face, I remember.
It is not your dancing, race-horse feet.
It is something else I remember you for on the pier
    mornings.

Your hands are sweeter than nut-brown bread when
    you touch me.
Your shoulder brushes my arm—a south-west wind
    crosses the pier.
I forget your hands and your shoulder and I say again:

Nothing else in this song—only your face.
Nothing else here—only your drinking, night-gray
    eyes.

LAUGHING BLUE STEEL

Two fishes swimming in the sea,
Two birds flying in the air,
Two chisels on an anvil—maybe.
Beaten, hammered, laughing blue steel to each other
    —maybe.
Sure I would rather be a chisel with you
                    than a fish.
Sure I would rather be a chisel with you
                    than a bird.
Take these two chisel-pals, O God.
Take 'em and beat 'em, hammer 'em,
                hear 'em laugh.

THEY ASK EACH OTHER WHERE THEY CAME FROM

Am I the river your white birds fly over?
Are you the green valley my silver channels roam?
The two of us a bowl of blue sky day time
        and a bowl of red stars night time?
    Who picked you
    out of the first great whirl of nothings
    and threw you here?

HOW MUCH?

How much do you love me, a million bushels?
Oh, a lot more than that, Oh, a lot more.

And to-morrow maybe only half a bushel?
To-morrow maybe not even a half a bushel.

And is this your heart arithmetic?
This is the way the wind measures the weather.

THROWBACKS

SOMEWHERE you and I remember we came.
Stairways from the sea and our heads dripping.
Ladders of dust and mud and our hair snarled.
Rags of drenching mist and our hands clawing, climb-
    ing.
You and I that snickered in the crotches and corners,
            in the gab of our first talking.
Red dabs of dawn summer mornings and the rain
    sliding off our shoulders summer afternoons.
Was it you and I yelled songs and songs in the nights
            of big yellow moons?

WIND SONG

LONG ago I learned how to sleep,
In an old apple orchard where the wind swept by
counting its money and throwing it away,
In a wind-gaunt orchard where the limbs forked out
and listened or never listened at all,
In a passel of trees where the branches trapped the
wind into whistling, "Who, who are you?"
I slept with my head in an elbow on a summer after-
noon and there I took a sleep lesson.
There I went away saying: I know why they sleep,
I know how they trap the tricky winds.
Long ago I learned how to listen to the singing wind
and how to forget and how to hear the deep
whine,
Slapping and lapsing under the day blue and the night
stars:
Who, who are you?

Who can ever forget
listening to the wind go by
counting its money
and throwing it away?

THREE SPRING NOTATIONS ON BIPEDS

1

THE down drop of the blackbird,
The wing catch of arrested flight,
The stop midway and then off:
    off for triangles, circles, loops
    of new hieroglyphs—
This is April's way: a woman:
" O yes, I'm here again and your heart
    knows I was coming."

2

White pigeons rush at the sun,
A marathon of wing feats is on:
" Who most loves danger? Who most loves
    wings? Who somersaults for God's sake
    in the name of wing power
    in the sun and blue
    on an April Thursday."
So ten winged heads, ten winged feet,
    race their white forms over Elmhurst.
They go fast: once the ten together were
    a feather of foam bubble, a chrysanthemum
    whirl speaking to silver and azure.

3

The child is on my shoulders.
In the prairie moonlight the child's legs
    hang over my shoulders.
She sits on my neck and I hear her calling
    me a good horse.
She slides down—and into the moon silver of
    a prairie stream
She throws a stone and laughs at the clug-clug.

SANDHILL PEOPLE

I TOOK away three pictures.
One was a white gull forming a half-mile arch from
the pines toward Waukegan.
One was a whistle in the little sandhills, a bird crying
either to the sunset gone or the dusk come.
One was three spotted waterbirds, zigzagging, cutting
scrolls and jags, writing a bird Sanscrit of wing
points, half over the sand, half over the water,
a half-love for the sea, a half-love for the land.

I took away three thoughts.
One was a thing my people call " love," a shut-in river
hunting the sea, breaking white falls between tall
clefs of hill country.
One was a thing my people call " silence," the wind
running over the butter faced sand-flowers, running over the sea, and never heard of again.
One was a thing my people call " death," neither a
whistle in the little sandhills, nor a bird Sanscrit
of wing points, yet a coat all the stars and seas
have worn, yet a face the beach wears between
sunset and dusk.

FAR ROCKAWAY NIGHT TILL MORNING

WHAT can we say of the night?
The fog night, the moon night,
   the fog moon night last night?

There swept out of the sea a song.
There swept out of the sea—
   torn white plungers.
There came on the coast wind drive
In the spit of a driven spray,
On the boom of foam and rollers,
The cry of midnight to morning:

   Hoi-a-loa.
   Hoi-a-loa.
   Hoi-a-loa.

Who has loved the night more than I have?
Who has loved the fog moon night last night
   more than I have?

Out of the sea that song
   —can I ever forget it?
Out of the sea those plungers
   —can I remember anything else?
Out of the midnight morning cry: Hoi-a-loa:
   —how can I hunt any other songs now?

HUMMINGBIRD WOMAN

WHY should I be wondering
How you would look in black velvet and yellow?
      in orange and green?
I who cannot remember whether it was a dash of blue
Or a whirr of red under your willow throat—
Why do I wonder how you would look in humming-
    bird feathers?

BUCKWHEAT

1

THERE was a late autumn cricket,
And two smoldering mountain sunsets
Under the valley roads of her eyes.

There was a late autumn cricket,
A hangover of summer song,
Scraping a tune
Of the late night clocks of summer,
In the late winter night fireglow,
This in a circle of black velvet at her neck.

2

In pansy eyes a flash, a thin rim of white light, a
    beach bonfire ten miles across dunes, a speck of
    a fool star in night's half circle of velvet.

In the corner of the left arm a dimple, a mole, a
    forget-me-not, and it fluttered a hummingbird
    wing, a blur in the honey-red clover, in the honey-
    white buckwheat.

BLUE RIDGE

BORN a million years ago you stay here a million
    years . . . watching the women come and live
    and be laid away . . . you and they thin-gray
    thin-dusk lovely.
So it goes: either the early morning lights are lovely
    or the early morning star.
I am glad I have seen racehorses, women, mountains.

VALLEY SONG

THE sunset swept
To the valley's west, you remember.

The frost was on.
A star burnt blue.
We were warm, you remember,
And counted the rings on a moon.

The sunset swept
To the valley's west
And was gone in a big dark door of stars.

MIST FORMS

THE sheets of night mist travel a long valley.
I know why you came at sundown in a scarf mist.

What was it we touched asking nothing and asking all?
How many times can death come and pay back what
    we saw?

In the oath of the sod, the lips that swore,
In the oath of night mist, nothing and all,
A riddle is here no man tells, no woman.

PIGEON

THE flutter of blue pigeon's wings
Under a river bridge
Hunting a clean dry arch,
A corner for a sleep—
This flutters here in a woman's hand.

A singing sleep cry,
A drunken poignant two lines of song,
Somebody looking clean into yesterday
And remembering, or looking clean into
To-morrow, and reading,—
This sings here as a woman's sleep cry sings.

Pigeon friend of mine,
Fly on, sing on.

CHASERS

THE sea at its worst drives a white foam up,
The same sea sometimes so easy and rocking with
    green mirrors.
So you were there when the white foam was up
And the salt spatter and the rack and the dulse—
You were done fingering these, and high, higher and
    higher
Your feet went and it was your voice went, " Hai,
    hai, hai,"
Up where the rocks let nothing live and the grass was
    gone,
Not even a hank nor a wisp of sea moss hoping.
Here your feet and your same singing, " Hai, hai, hai."

Was there anything else to answer than, " Hai, hai,
    hai "?
Did I go up those same crags yesterday and the day
    before
Scruffing my shoe leather and scraping the tough
    gnomic stuff
Of stones woven on a cold criss-cross so long ago?
Have I not sat there . . . watching the white foam up,
The hoarse white lines coming to curve, foam, slip
    back?
Didn't I learn then how the call comes, " Hai, hai,
    hai "?

HORSE FIDDLE

First I would like to write for you a poem to be
    shouted in the teeth of a strong wind.
Next I would like to write one for you to sit on a
    hill and read down the river valley on a late
    summer afternoon, reading it in less than a whis-
    per to Jack on his soft wire legs learning to stand
    up and preach, Jack-in-the-pulpit.
As many poems as I have written to the moon and
    the streaming of the moon spinners of light, so
    many of the summer moon and the winter moon I
    would like to shoot along to your ears for nothing,
    for a laugh, a song,
                for nothing at all,
                for one look from you,
                for your face turned away
                and your voice in one clutch
                half way between a tree wind moan
                and a night-bird sob.
Believe nothing of it all, pay me nothing, open your
    window for the other singers and keep it shut
    for me.
The road I am on is a long road and I can go hungry
    again like I have gone hungry before.
What else have I done nearly all my life than go
    hungry and go on singing?

Leave me with the hoot owl.
I have slept in a blanket listening.
He learned it, he must have learned it
From two moons, the summer moon,
And the winter moon
And the streaming of the moon spinners of light.

TIMBER WINGS

THERE was a wild pigeon came often to Hinkley's
  timber.
Gray wings that wrote their loops and triangles on
  the walnuts and the hazel.
      There was a wild pigeon.

There was a summer came year by year to Hinkley's
  timber.
Rainy months and sunny and pigeons calling and one
  pigeon best of all who came.
      There was a summer.

It is so long ago I saw this wild pigeon and listened.
It is so long ago I heard the summer song of the
  pigeon who told me why night comes, why death
  and stars come, why the whippoorwill remembers
  three notes only and always.
It is so long ago; it is like now and today; the gray
  wing pigeon's way of telling it all, telling it to the
  walnuts and hazel, telling it to me.
      So there is memory.
      So there is a pigeon, a summer, a gray wing
  beating my shoulder.

NIGHT STUFF

LISTEN a while, the moon is a lovely woman, a lonely
woman, lost in a silver dress, lost in a circus
rider's silver dress.

Listen a while, the lake by night is a lonely woman, a
lovely woman, circled with birches and pines mixing their green and white among stars shattered
in spray clear nights.

I know the moon and the lake have twisted the roots
under my heart the same as a lonely woman, a
lovely woman, in a silver dress, in a circus rider's
silver dress.

SPANISH

FASTEN black eyes on me.
I ask nothing of you under the peach trees,
Fasten your black eyes in my gray
      with the spear of a storm.
The air under the peach blossoms is a haze of pink.

SHAG-BARK HICKORY

IN the moonlight under a shag-bark hickory tree
Watching the yellow shadows melt in hoof-pools,
Listening to the yes and the no of a woman's hands,
I kept my guess why the night was glad.

The night was lit with a woman's eyes.
The night was crossed with a woman's hands,
The night kept humming an undersong.

THE SOUTH WIND SAYS SO

If the oriole calls like last year
when the south wind sings in the oats,
if the leaves climb and climb on a bean pole
saying over a song learnt from the south wind,
if the crickets send up the same old lessons
found when the south wind keeps on coming,
we will get by, we will keep on coming,
we will get by, we will come along,
we will fix our hearts over,
the south wind says so.

ACCOMPLISHED FACTS

ACCOMPLISHED FACTS

EVERY year Emily Dickinson sent one friend
the first arbutus bud in her garden.

In a last will and testament Andrew Jackson
remembered a friend with the gift of George
Washington's pocket spy-glass.

Napoleon too, in a last testament, mentioned a silver
watch taken from the bedroom of Frederick the Great,
and passed along this trophy to a particular friend.

O. Henry took a blood carnation from his coat lapel
and handed it to a country girl starting work in a
bean bazaar, and scribbled: " Peach blossoms may or
may not stay pink in city dust."

So it goes.   Some things we buy, some not.
Tom Jefferson was proud of his radishes, and Abe
Lincoln blacked his own boots, and Bismarck called
Berlin a wilderness of brick and newspapers.

So it goes.   There are accomplished facts.
Ride, ride, ride on in the great new blimps—
Cross unheard-of oceans, circle the planet.
When you come back we may sit by five hollyhocks.
We might listen to boys fighting for marbles.
The grasshopper will look good to us.

So it goes . . .

GRIEG BEING DEAD

GRIEG being dead we may speak of him and his art.
Grieg being dead we can talk about whether he was
    any good or not.
Grieg being with Ibsen, Björnson, Lief Ericson and
    the rest,
Grieg being dead does not care a hell's hoot what
    we say.

Morning, Spring, Anitra's Dance,
He dreams them at the doors of new stars.

CHORDS

In the morning, a Sunday morning, shadows of sea
and adumbrants of rock in her eyes . . . horseback in leather boots and leather gauntlets by
the sea.

In the evening, a Sunday evening, a rope of pearls
on her white shoulders . . . and a speaking,
brooding black velvet, relapsing to the voiceless
. . . battering Russian marches on a piano . . .
drive of blizzards across Nebraska.

Yes, riding horseback on hills by the sea . . . sitting
at the ivory keys in black velvet, a rope of pearls
on white shoulders.

DOGHEADS

Among the grassroots
In the moonlight, who comes circling,
    red tongues and high noses?
Is one of 'em Buck and one of 'em
    White Fang?

In the moonlight, who are they, cross-legged,
    telling their stories over and over?
Is one of 'em Martin Eden and one of 'em Larsen
    the Wolf?

Let an epitaph read:
    He loved the straight eyes of dogs
    and the strong heads of men.

TRINITY PEACE

THE grave of Alexander Hamilton is in Trinity yard
at the end of Wall Street.

The grave of Robert Fulton likewise is in Trinity
yard where Wall Street stops.

And in this yard stenogs, bundle boys, scrubwomen,
sit on the tombstones, and walk on the grass of
graves, speaking of war and weather, of babies,
wages and love.

An iron picket fence . . . and streaming thousands
along Broadway sidewalks . . . straw hats,
faces, legs . . . a singing, talking, hustling river
. . . down the great street that ends with a Sea.

. . . easy is the sleep of Alexander Hamilton.
. . . easy is the sleep of Robert Fulton.
. . . easy are the great governments and the great
steamboats.

PORTRAIT

(*For S. A.*)

To write one book in five years
or five books in one year,
to be the painter and the thing painted,
. . . where are we, bo?

Wait—get his number.
The barber shop handling is here
and the tweeds, the cheviot, the Scotch Mist,
and the flame orange scarf.

Yet there is more—he sleeps under bridges
with lonely crazy men; he sits in country
jails with bootleggers; he adopts the children
of broken-down burlesque actresses; he has
cried a heart of tears for Windy MacPherson's
father; he pencils wrists of lonely women.

Can a man sit at a desk in a skyscraper in Chicago
and be a harnessmaker in a corn town in Iowa
and feel the tall grass coming up in June
and the ache of the cottonwood trees
singing with the prairie wind?

POTOMAC RIVER MIST

ALL the policemen, saloonkeepers and efficiency experts in Toledo knew Bern Dailey; secretary ten years when Whitlock was mayor.
Pickpockets, yeggs, three card men, he knew them all and how they flit from zone to zone, birds of wind and weather, singers, fighters, scavengers.

The Washington monument pointed to a new moon for us and a gang from over the river sang ragtime to a ukelele.
The river mist marched up and down the Potomac, we hunted the fog-swept Lincoln Memorial, white as a blond woman's arm.
We circled the city of Washington and came back home four o'clock in the morning, passing a sign: House Where Abraham Lincoln Died, Admission 25 Cents.

I got a letter from him in Sweden and I sent him a postcard from Norway . . every newspaper from America ran news of " the flu."

The path of a night fog swept up the river to the Lincoln Memorial when I saw it again and alone at a winter's end, the marble in the mist white as a blond woman's arm.

JACK LONDON AND O. HENRY

BOTH were jailbirds; no speechmakers at all;
speaking best with one foot on a brass rail;
a beer glass in the left hand and the right
hand employed for gestures.

And both were lights snuffed out . . . no warning
. . . no lingering:

Who knew the hearts of these boozefighters?

HIS OWN FACE HIDDEN

Hokusai's portrait of himself
Tells what his hat was like
And his arms and legs. The only faces
Are a river and a mountain
And two laughing farmers.

The smile of Hokusai
is under his hat.

CUPS OF COFFEE

THE haggard woman with a hacking cough and a
deathless love whispers of white flowers . . . in
your poem you pour like a cup of coffee, Gabriel.

The slim girl whose voice was lost in the waves of
flesh piled on her bones . . . and the woman who
sold to many men and saw her breasts shrivel
. . . in two poems you pour these like a cup of
coffee, Francois.

The woman whose lips are a thread of scarlet, the
woman whose feet take hold on hell, the woman
who turned to a memorial of salt looking at the
lights of a forgotten city . . . in your affidavits,
ancient Jews, you pour these like cups of coffee.

The woman who took men as snakes take rabbits, a
rag and a bone and a hank of hair, she whose
eyes called men to sea dreams and shark's teeth
. . . in a poem you pour this like a cup of coffee,
Kip.

Marching to the footlights in night robes with spots
of blood, marching in white sheets muffling the
faces, marching with heads in the air they come
back and cough and cry and sneer: . . . in your
poems, men, you pour these like cups of coffee.

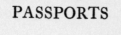

PASSPORTS

SMOKE ROSE GOLD

THE dome of the capitol looks to the Potomac river.
    Out of haze over the sunset,
    Out of a smoke rose gold:
One star shines over the sunset.
Night takes the dome and the river, the sun and the
    smoke rose gold,
The haze changes from sunset to star.
The pour of a thin silver struggles against the dark.
A star might call: It's a long way across.

TANGIBLES
(*Washington, August,* 1918)

I HAVE seen this city in the day and the sun.
I have seen this city in the night and the moon.
And in the night and the moon I have seen a thing this
city gave me nothing of in the day and the sun.

The float of the dome in the day and the sun is one
thing.
The float of the dome in the night and the moon is
another thing.
In the night and the moon the float of the dome is a
dream-whisper, a croon of a hope: "Not today,
child, not today, lover; maybe tomorrow, child,
maybe tomorrow, lover."

Can a dome of iron dream deeper than living men?
Can the float of a shape hovering among tree-tops—
can this speak an oratory sad, singing and red
beyond the speech of the living men?

A mother of men, a sister, a lover, a woman past the
dreams of the living—
Does she go sad, singing and red out of the float of
this dome?

There is . . . something . . . here . . . men die for.

NIGHT MOVEMENT—NEW YORK

In the night, when the sea-winds take the city in their
arms,
And cool the loud streets that kept their dust noon and
afternoon;
In the night, when the sea-birds call to the lights of
the city,
The lights that cut on the skyline their name of a city;
In the night, when the trains and wagons start from
a long way off
For the city where the people ask bread and want
letters;
In the night the city lives too—the day is not all.
In the night there are dancers dancing and singers
singing,
And the sailors and soldiers look for numbers on doors.
In the night the sea-winds take the city in their arms.

NORTH ATLANTIC

WHEN the sea is everywhere
from horizon to horizon . .
  when the salt and blue
  fill a circle of horizons . .
I swear again how I know
the sea is older than anything else
and the sea younger than anything else.

My first father was a landsman.
My tenth father was a sea-lover,
  a gipsy sea-boy, a singer of chanties.
  (Oh Blow the Man Down!)

The sea is always the same:
and yet the sea always changes.

    The sea gives all,
    and yet the sea keeps something back.

The sea takes without asking.
The sea is a worker, a thief and a loafer.
    Why does the sea let go so slow?
    Or never let go at all?

  The sea always the same
  day after day,
  the sea always the same

night after night,
fog on fog and never a star,
wind on wind and running white sheets,
bird on bird always a sea-bird—
so the days get lost:
it is neither Saturday nor Monday,
it is any day or no day,
it is a year, ten years.

Fog on fog and never a star,
what is a man, a child, a woman,
to the green and grinding sea?
The ropes and boards squeak and groan.

On the land they know a child they have named Today.
On the sea they know three children they have named:
Yesterday, Today, To-morrow.

I made a song to a woman:—it ran:
I have wanted you.
I have called to you
on a day I counted a thousand years.

In the deep of a sea-blue noon
many women run in a man's head,
phantom women leaping from a man's forehead
. . to the railings . . . into the sea . . . to the
sea rim . . .
. . a man's mother . . . a man's wife . . . other
women . . .
I asked a sure-footed sailor how and he said:
I have known many women but there is only one sea.

I saw the North Star once
and our old friend, The Big Dipper,
  only the sea between us:
  " Take away the sea
  and I lift The Dipper,
  swing the handle of it,
  drink from the brim of it."

I saw the North Star one night
and five new stars for me in the rigging ropes,
and seven old stars in the cross of the wireless
            plunging by night,
            plowing by night—
Five new cool stars, seven old warm stars.

I have been let down in a thousand graves
            by my kinfolk.
I have been left alone with the sea and the sea's
  wife, the wind, for my last friends
And my kinfolk never knew anything about it at all.

Salt from an old work of eating our graveclothes is
    here.
  The sea-kin of my thousand graves,
  The sea and the sea's wife, the wind,
They are all here to-night
            between the circle of horizons,
            between the cross of the wireless
            and the seven old warm stars.

Out of a thousand sea-holes I came yesterday.
Out of a thousand sea-holes I come to-morrow.

I am kin of the changer.
        I am a son of the sea
          and the sea's wife, the wind.

FOG PORTRAIT

RINGS of iron gray smoke; a woman's steel face . . . looking . . . looking.

Funnels of an ocean liner negotiating a fog night; pouring a taffy mass down the wind; layers of soot on the top deck; a taffrail . . . and a woman's steel face . . . looking . . . looking.

Cliffs challenge humped; sudden arcs form on a gull's wing in the storm's vortex; miles of white horses plow through a stony beach; stars, clear sky, and everywhere free climbers calling; and a woman's steel face . . . looking . . . looking . . .

FLYING FISH

I HAVE lived in many half-worlds myself . . . and
so I know you.

I leaned at a deck rail watching a monotonous sea, the
same circling birds and the same plunge of furrows carved by the plowing keel.

I leaned so . . . and you fluttered struggling between
two waves in the air now . . . and then under
the water and out again . . . a fish . . . a bird
. . . a fin thing . . . a wing thing.

Child of water, child of air, fin thing and wing thing
. . . I have lived in many half worlds myself . . .
and so I know you.

HOME THOUGHTS

THE sea rocks have a green moss.
The pine rocks have red berries.
I have memories of you.

. . . .

Speak to me of how you miss me.
Tell me the hours go long and slow.

Speak to me of the drag on your heart,
The iron drag of the long days.

I know hours empty as a beggar's tin cup on a rainy
  day, empty as a soldier's sleeve with an arm lost.

Speak to me . . .

IN THE SHADOW OF THE PALACE

LET us go out of the fog, John, out of the filmy per-
sistent drizzle on the streets of Stockholm, let
us put down the collars of our raincoats, take
off our hats and sit in the newspaper office.

Let us sit among the telegrams—clickety-click—the
kaiser's crown goes into the gutter and the Hohen-
zollern throne of a thousand years falls to pieces
a one-hoss shay.

It is a fog night out and the umbrellas are up and
the collars of the raincoats—and all the steamboats up and down the Baltic sea have their lights
out and the wheelsmen sober.

Here the telegrams come—one king goes and another
—butter is costly: there is no butter to buy for
our bread in Stockholm—and a little patty of
butter costs more than all the crowns of Germany.

Let us go out in the fog, John, let us roll up our
raincoat collars and go on the streets where men
are sneering at the kings.

TWO ITEMS

STRONG rocks hold up the riksdag bridge . . . always
strong river waters shoving their shoulders against
them . . .

In the riksdag to-night three hundred men are talking
to each other about more potatoes and bread for
the Swedish people to eat this winter.

In a boat among calm waters next to the running
waters a fisherman sits in the dark and I, leaning
at a parapet, see him lift a net and let it down
. . . he waits . . . the waters run . . . the
riksdag talks . . . he lifts the net and lets it
down . . .

Stars lost in the sky ten days of drizzle spread over
the sky saying yes-yes.

. . . .

Every afternoon at four o'clock fifteen apple women
who have sold their apples in Christiania meet
at a coffee house and gab.

Every morning at nine o'clock a girl wipes the windows of a hotel across the street from the postoffice in Stockholm.

I have pledged them when I go to California next
summer and see the orange groves splattered with
yellow balls

I shall remember other people half way round the
world.

STREETS TOO OLD

I WALKED among the streets of an old city and the streets were lean as the throats of hard seafish soaked in salt and kept in barrels many years.

How old, how old, how old, we are:—the walls went on saying, street walls leaning toward each other like old women of the people, like old midwives tired and only doing what must be done.

The greatest the city could offer me, a stranger, was statues of the kings, on all corners bronzes of kings—ancient bearded kings who wrote books and spoke of God's love for all people—and young kings who took forth armies out across the frontiers splitting the heads of their opponents and enlarging their kingdoms.

Strangest of all to me, a stranger in this old city, was the murmur always whistling on the winds twisting out of the armpits and fingertips of the kings in bronze:—Is there no loosening? Is this for always?

In an early snowflurry one cried:—Pull me down where the tired old midwives no longer look at me, throw the bronze of me to a fierce fire and make me into neckchains for dancing children.

SAVOIR FAIRE

CAST a bronze of my head and legs and put them on
the king's street.

Set the cast of me here alongside Carl XII, making
two Carls for the Swedish people and the utlanders
to look at between the palace and the Grand
Hotel.

The summer sun will shine on both the Carls, and
November drizzles wrap the two, one in tall
leather boots, one in wool leggins.

Also I place it in the record: the Swedish people may
name boats after me or change the name of a
long street and give it one of my nicknames.

The old men who beset the soil of Sweden and own
the titles to the land—the old men who enjoy a
silken shimmer to their chin whiskers when they
promenade the streets named after old kings—
if they forget me—the old men whose varicose
veins stand more and more blue on the calves of
their legs when they take their morning baths
attended by old women born to the bath service
of old men and young—if these old men say
another King Carl should have a bronze on the
king's street rather than a Fool Carl—

Then I would hurl them only another fool's laugh—

I would remember last Sunday when I stood on a
jutland of fire-born red granite watching the
drop of the sun in the middle of the afternoon and
the full moon shining over Stockholm four o'clock
in the afternoon.

If the young men will read five lines of one of my
poems I will let the kings have all the bronze—
I ask only that one page of my writings be a
knapsack keepsake of the young men who are the
bloodkin of those who laughed nine hundred years
ago: We are afraid of nothing—only—the sky
may fall on us.

MOHAMMED BEK HADJETLACHE

THIS Mohammedan colonel from the Caucasus yells
with his voice and wigwags with his arms.

The interpreter translates, " I was a friend of Korni-
lov, he asks me what to do and I tell him."

A stub of a man, this Mohammedan colonel . . . a
projectile shape . . . a bald head hammered . . .

" Does he fight or do they put him in a cannon and
shoot him at the enemy?"

This fly-by-night, this bull-roarer who knows everybody.

" I write forty books, history of Islam, history of
Europe, true religion, scientific farming, I am
the Roosevelt of the Caucasus, I go to America
and ride horses in the moving pictures for $500,-
000, you get $50,000 . . ."

" I have 30,000 acres in the Caucasus, I have a stove
factory in Petrograd the bolsheviks take from
me, I am an old friend of the Czar, I am an old
family friend of Clemenceau . . ."

These hands strangled three fellow workers for the
czarist restoration, took their money, sent them
in sacks to a river bottom . . . and scandalized
Stockholm with his gang of strangler women.

Mid-sea strangler hands rise before me illustrating a
wish, " I ride horses for the moving pictures in
America, $500,000, and you get ten per cent . . ."

This rider of fugitive dawns. . . . .

HIGH CONSPIRATORIAL PERSONS

OUT of the testimony of such reluctant lips, out of
the oaths and mouths of such scrupulous liars,
out of perjurers whose hands swore by God to
the white sun before all men,

Out of a rag saturated with smears and smuts gathered from the footbaths of kings and the loin
cloths of whores, from the scabs of Babylon and
Jerusalem to the scabs of London and New York,

From such a rag that has wiped the secret sores of
kings and overlords across the milleniums of
human marches and babblings,

From such a rag perhaps I shall wring one reluctant
desperate drop of blood, one honest-to-God spot
of red speaking a mother-heart.
December, 1918.
Christiania, Norway

BALTIC FOG NOTES

(Bergen)

SEVEN days all fog, all mist, and the turbines pounding through high seas.
I was a plaything, a rat's neck in the teeth of a scuffling
 mastiff.
Fog and fog and no stars, sun, moon.
Then an afternoon in fjords, low-lying lands scrawled
 in granite languages on a gray sky,
A night harbor, blue dusk mountain shoulders against
 a night sky,
And a circle of lights blinking: Ninety thousand
 people here.

> Among the Wednesday night thousands in
> goloshes and coats slickered for rain,
> I learned how hungry I was for streets and
> people.

. . . .

I would rather be water than anything else.
I saw a drive of salt fog and mist in the North Atlantic
 and an iceberg dusky as a cloud in the gray of
 morning.
And I saw the dream pools of fjords in Norway . . .
 and the scarf of dancing water on the rocks and
 over the edges of mountain shelves.

. . . .

Bury me in a mountain graveyard in Norway.
Three tongues of water sing around it with snow
from the mountains.

Bury me in the North Atlantic.
A fog there from Iceland will be a murmur in gray
over me and a long deep wind sob always.

Bury me in an Illinois cornfield.
The blizzards loosen their pipe organ voluntaries in
winter stubble and the spring rains and the fall
rains bring letters from the sea.

CIRCLES OF DOORS

CIRCLES OF DOORS

I LOVE him, I love him, ran the patter of her lips
And she formed his name on her tongue and sang
And she sent him word she loved him so much,
So much, and death was nothing; work, art, home,
All was nothing if her love for him was not first
Of all; the patter of her lips ran, I love him,
I love him; and he knew the doors that opened
Into doors and more doors, no end of doors,
And full length mirrors doubling and tripling
The apparitions of doors: circling corridors of
Looking glasses and doors, some with knobs, some
With no knobs, some opening slow to a heavy push,
And some jumping open at a touch and a hello.
And he knew if he so wished he could follow her
Swift running through circles of doors, hearing
Sometimes her whisper, I love him, I love him,
And sometimes only a high chaser of laughter
Somewhere five or ten doors ahead or five or ten
Doors behind, or chittering *h-st, h-st,* among corners
Of the tall full-length dusty looking glasses.
I love, I love, I love, she sang short and quick in
High thin beaten soprano and he knew the meanings,
The high chaser of laughter, the doors on doors
And the looking glasses, the room to room hunt,
The ends opening into new ends always.

HATE

ONE man killed another. The saying between them
   had been " I'd give you the shirt off my back."

The killer wept over the dead. The dead if he looks
   back knows the killer was sorry. It was a shot
   in one second of hate out of ten years of love.

Why is the sun a red ball in the six o'clock mist?
Why is the moon a tumbling chimney? . . . tumbling
   . . . tumbling . . . " I'd give you the shirt off
   my back " . . . And I'll kill you if my head
   goes wrong.

TWO STRANGERS BREAKFAST

THE law says you and I belong to each other, George.
The law says you are mine and I am yours, George.
And there are a million miles of white snowstorms, a
    million furnaces of hell,
Between the chair where you sit and the chair where
    I sit.
The law says two strangers shall eat breakfast together
    after nights on the horn of an Arctic moon.

SNOW

Snow took us away from the smoke valleys into white mountains, we saw velvet blue cows eating a vermillion grass and they gave us a pink milk.

Snow changes our bones into fog streamers caught by the wind and spelled into many dances.

Six bits for a sniff of snow in the old days bought us bubbles beautiful to forget floating long arm women across sunny autumn hills.

Our bones cry and cry, no let-up, cry their telegrams: More, more—a yen is on, a long yen and God only knows when it will end.

In the old days six bits got us snow and stopped the yen—now the government says: No, no, when our bones cry their telegrams: More, more.

The blue cows are dying, no more pink milk, no more floating long arm women, the hills are empty— us for the smoke valleys—sneeze and shiver and croak, you dopes—the government says: No, no.

DANCER

The lady in red, she in the chile con carne red,
Brilliant as the shine of a pepper crimson in the
summer sun,
She behind a false-face, the much sought-after dancer,
the most sought-after dancer of all in this mas-
querade,
The lady in red sox and red hat, ankles of willow,
crimson arrow amidst the Spanish clashes of
music,

I sit in a corner
watching her dance first with one man
and then another.

PLASTER

"I KNEW a real man once," says Agatha in the splendor of a shagbark hickory tree.

Did a man touch his lips to Agatha? Did a man hold her in his arms? Did a man only look at her and pass by?

Agatha, far past forty in a splendor of remembrance, says, "I knew a real man once."

CURSE OF A RICH POLISH PEASANT ON HIS SISTER WHO RAN AWAY WITH A WILD MAN

FELIKSOWA has gone again from our house and this time for good, I hope.

She and her husband took with them the cow father gave them, and they sold it.

She went like a swine, because she called neither on me, her brother, nor on her father, before leaving for those forests.

That is where she ought to live, with bears, not with men.

She was something of an ape before and there, with her wild husband, she became altogether an ape.

No honest person would have done as they did.

Whose fault is it? And how much they have cursed me and their father!

May God not punish them for it. They think only about money; they let the church go if they can only live fat on their money.

WOMAN WITH A PAST

THERE was a woman tore off a red velvet gown
And slashed the white skin of her right shoulder
And a crimson zigzag wrote a finger nail hurry.

There was a woman spoke six short words
And quit a life that was old to her
For a life that was new.

There was a woman swore an oath
And gave hoarse whisper to a prayer
And it was all over.

She was a thief and a whore and a kept woman,
She was a thing to be used and played with.
She wore an ancient scarlet sash.

The story is thin and wavering,
White as a face in the first apple blossoms,
White as a birch in the snow of a winter moon.

The story is never told.
There are white lips whisper alone.
There are red lips whisper alone.

In the cool of the old walls,
In the white of the old walls,
The red song is over.

WHITE HANDS

FOR the second time in a year this lady with the white
hands is brought to the west room second floor
of a famous sanatorium.

Her husband is a cornice manufacturer in an Iowa
town and the lady has often read papers on Vic-
torian poets before the local literary club.

Yesterday she washed her hands forty seven times
during her waking hours and in her sleep moaned
restlessly attempting to clean imaginary soiled
spots off her hands.

Now the head physician touches his chin with a
crooked forefinger.

AN ELECTRIC SIGN GOES DARK

POLAND, France, Judea ran in her veins,
Singing to Paris for bread, singing to Gotham in a
    fizz at the pop of a bottle's cork.

" Won't you come and play wiz me " she sang . . . and
    " I just can't make my eyes behave."
" Higgeldy-Piggeldy," " Papa's Wife," " Follow Me "
    were plays.

Did she wash her feet in a tub of milk? Was a strand
    of pearls sneaked from her trunk? The news-
    papers asked.
Cigarettes, tulips, pacing horses, took her name.

Twenty years old . . . thirty . . . forty . . .
Forty-five and the doctors fathom nothing, the doctors
    quarrel, the doctors use silver tubes feeding
    twenty-four quarts of blood into the veins, the
    respects of a prize-fighter, a cab driver.
And a little mouth moans: It is easy to die when they
    are dying so many grand deaths in France.

A voice, a shape, gone.
A baby bundle from Warsaw . . . legs, torso, head
    . . . on a hotel bed at The Savoy.

The white chiselings of flesh that flung themselves in
  somersaults, straddles, for packed houses:
A memory, a stage and footlights out, an electric sign
  on Broadway dark.

She belonged to somebody, nobody.
No one man owned her, no ten nor a thousand.
She belonged to many thousand men, lovers of the
  white chiseling of arms and shoulders, the ivory
  of a laugh, the bells of song.

Railroad brakemen taking trains across Nebraska
  prairies, lumbermen jaunting in pine and tamarack
  of the Northwest, stock ranchers in the middle
  west, mayors of southern cities
Say to their pals and wives now: I see by the papers
  Anna Held is dead.

THEY BUY WITH AN EYE TO LOOKS

THE fine cloth of your love might be a fabric of Egypt,
Something Sinbad, the sailor, took away from robbers,
Something a traveler with plenty of money might
    pick up
And bring home and stick on the walls and say:
" There's a little thing made a hit with me
When I was in Cairo—I think I must see Cairo again
    some day."
So there are cornice manufacturers, chewing gum
    kings,
Young Napoleons who corner eggs or corner cheese,
Phenoms looking for more worlds to corner,
And still other phenoms who lard themselves in
And make a killing in steel, copper, permanganese,
And they say to random friends in for a call:
" Have you had a look at my wife? Here she is.
  Haven't I got her dolled up for fair?"
O-ee! the fine cloth of your love might be a fabric of
    Egypt.

PROUD AND BEAUTIFUL

AFTER you have spent all the money modistes and
manicures and mannikins will take for fixing you
over into a thing the people on the streets call
proud and beautiful,

After the shops and fingers have worn out all they
have and know and can hope to have and know
for the sake of making you what the people on
the streets call proud and beautiful,

After there is absolutely nothing more to be done for
the sake of staging you as a great enigmatic bird
of paradise and they must all declare you to be
proud and beautiful,

After you have become the last word in good looks,
insofar as good looks may be fixed and formu-
lated, then, why then, there is nothing more to
it then, it is then you listen and see how voices
and eyes declare you to be proud and beautiful.

TELEGRAM

I SAW a telegram handed a two hundred pound man
at a desk. And the little scrap of paper charged
the air like a set of crystals in a chemist's tube
to a whispering pinch of salt.
Cross my heart, the two hundred pound man had just
cracked a joke about a new hat he got his wife,
when the messenger boy slipped in and asked
him to sign. He gave the boy a nickel, tore the
envelope and read.
Then he yelled "Good God," jumped for his hat and
raincoat, ran for the elevator and took a taxi
to a railroad depot.

As I say, it was like a set of crystals in a chemist's
tube and a whispering pinch of salt.
I wonder what Diogenes who lived in a tub in the
sun would have commented on the affair.
I know a shoemaker who works in a cellar slamming
half-soles onto shoes, and when I told him, he
said: "I pay my bills, I love my wife, and I am
not afraid of anybody."

GLIMMER

Let down your braids of hair, lady.
Cross your legs and sit before the looking-glass
And gaze long on lines under your eyes.
Life writes; men dance.
     And you know how men pay women.

WHITE ASH

THERE is a woman on Michigan Boulevard keeps a parrot and goldfish and two white mice.

She used to keep a houseful of girls in kimonos and three pushbuttons on the front door.

Now she is alone with a parrot and goldfish and two white mice . . . but these are some of her thoughts:

The love of a soldier on furlough or a sailor on shore leave burns with a bonfire red and saffron.

The love of an emigrant workman whose wife is a thousand miles away burns with a blue smoke.

The love of a young man whose sweetheart married an older man for money burns with a sputtering uncertain flame.

And there is a love . . . one in a thousand . . . burns clean and is gone leaving a white ash. . . .

And this is a thought she never explains to the parrot and goldfish and two white mice.

TESTIMONY REGARDING A GHOST

The roses slanted crimson sobs
On the night sky hair of the women,
And the long light-fingered men
Spoke to the dark-haired women,
"Nothing lovelier, nothing lovelier."
How could he sit there among us all
Guzzling blood into his guts,
Goblets, mugs, buckets—
Leaning, toppling, laughing
With a slobber on his mouth,
A smear of red on his strong raw lips,
How could he sit there
And only two or three of us see him?
        There was nothing to it.
He wasn't there at all, of course.

The roses leaned from the pots.
The sprays snot roses gold and red
And the roses slanted crimson sobs
        In the night sky hair
And the voices chattered on the way
To the frappe, speaking of pictures,
Speaking of a strip of black velvet
Crossing a girlish woman's throat,
Speaking of the mystic music flash
Of pots and sprays of roses,
"Nothing lovelier, nothing lovelier."

PUT OFF THE WEDDING FIVE TIMES AND NOBODY COMES TO IT

(Handbook for Quarreling Lovers)

I THOUGHT of offering you apothegms.

I might have said, "Dogs bark and the wind carries it away."

I might have said, "He who would make a door of gold must knock a nail in every day."

So easy, so easy it would have been to inaugurate a high impetuous moment for you to look on before the final farewells were spoken.

You who assumed the farewells in the manner of people buying newspapers and reading the headlines—and all peddlers of gossip who buttonhole each other and wag their heads saying, "Yes, I heard all about it last Wednesday."

I considered several apothegms.

"There is no love but service," of course, would only initiate a quarrel over who has served and how and when.

"Love stands against fire and flood and much bitterness," would only initiate a second misunderstanding, and bickerings with lapses of silence.

What is there in the Bible to cover our case, or Shakespere? What poetry can help? Is there any left but Epictetus?

Since you have already chosen to interpret silence for
language and silence for despair and silence for
contempt and silence for all things but love,
Since you have already chosen to read ashes where
God knows there was something else than ashes,
Since silence and ashes are two identical findings for
your eyes and there are no apothegms worth
handing out like a hung jury's verdict for a record
in our own hearts as well as the community at
large,
I can only remember a Russian peasant who told me
his grandfather warned him: If you ride too good
a horse you will not take the straight road to
town.

It will always come back to me in the blur of that
hokku: The heart of a woman of thirty is like
the red ball of the sun seen through a mist.
Or I will remember the witchery in the eyes of a girl
at a barn dance one winter night in Illinois saying:
Put off the wedding five times and nobody
comes to it.

BABY VAMPS

Baby vamps, is it harder work than it used to be?
Are the new soda parlors worse than the old time
     saloons?
  Baby vamps, do you have jobs in the day time
                or is this all you do?
                do you come out only at night?
In the winter at the skating rinks, in the summer at the
     roller coaster parks,
Wherever figure eights are carved, by skates in winter,
     by roller coasters in summer,
Wherever the whirligigs are going and chicken spanish
     and hot dog are sold,
There you come, giggling baby vamp, there you come
     with your blue baby eyes, saying:
          Take me along.

VAUDEVILLE DANCER

ELSIE FLIMMERWON, you got a job now with a jazz outfit in vaudeville.

The houses go wild when you finish the act shimmying a fast shimmy to The Livery Stable Blues.

It is long ago, Elsie Flimmerwon, I saw your mother over a washtub in a grape arbor when your father came with the locomotor ataxia shuffle.

It is long ago, Elsie, and now they spell your name with an electric sign.

Then you were a little thing in checked gingham and your mother wiped your nose and said: You little fool, keep off the streets.

Now you are a big girl at last and streetfuls of people read your name and a line of people shaped like a letter S stand at the box office hoping to see you shimmy.

BALLOON FACES

THE balloons hang on wires in the Marigold Gardens.
They spot their yellow and gold, they juggle their blue
   and red, they float their faces on the face of the
   sky.
Balloon face eaters sit by hundreds reading the eat
   cards, asking, "What shall we eat?"—and the
   waiters, "Have you ordered?" they are sixty
   ballon faces sifting white over the tuxedoes.
Poets, lawyers, ad men, mason contractors, smart-
   alecks discussing "educated jackasses," here they
   put crabs into their balloon faces.
Here sit the heavy balloon face women lifting crimson
   lobsters into their crimson faces, lobsters out of
   Sargossa sea bottoms.
Here sits a man cross-examining a woman, "Where
   were you last night? What do you do with all
   your money? Who's buying your shoes now,
   anyhow?"
So they sit eating whitefish, two balloon faces swept
   on God's night wind.
And all the time the balloon spots on the wires, a little
   mile of festoons, they play their own silence play
   of film yellow and film gold, bubble blue and bubble red.
The wind crosses the town, the wind from the west
   side comes to the banks of marigolds boxed in the
   Marigold Gardens.

Night moths fly and fix their feet in the leaves and
    eat and are seen by the eaters.

The jazz outfit sweats and the drums and the saxo-
    phones reach for the ears of the eaters.

The chorus brought from Broadway works at the fun
    and the slouch of their shoulders, the kick of their
    ankles, reach for the eyes of the eaters.

These girls from Kokomo and Peoria, these hungry
    girls, since they are paid-for, let us look on and
    listen, let us get their number.

Why do I go again to the balloons on the wires, some-
    thing for nothing, kin women of the half-moon,
    dream women?

And the half-moon swinging on the wind crossing the
    town—these two, the half-moon and the wind—
    this will be about all, this will be about all.

Eaters, go to it; your mazuma pays for it all; it's a
    knockout, a classy knockout—and payday always
    comes.

The moths in the marigolds will do for me, the half-
    moon, the wishing wind and the little mile of
    balloon spots on wires—this will be about all, this
    will be about all.

HAZE

criticize

HAZE

KEEP a red heart of memories
Under the great gray rain sheds of the sky,
Under the open sun and the yellow gloaming embers.
Remember all paydays of lilacs and songbirds;
All starlights of cool memories on storm paths.

Out of this prairie rise the faces of dead men.
They speak to me.   I can not tell you what they say.

Other faces rise on the prairie.
                    They are the unborn.   The future.

Yesterday and to-morrow cross and mix on the sky-
    line
The two are lost in a purple haze.   One forgets.   One
    waits.

In the yellow dust of sunsets, in the meadows of
    vermilion eight o'clock June nights . . . the
    dead men and the unborn children speak to me
    . . . I can not tell you what they say . . . you
    listen and you know.

I don't care who you are, man:
I know a woman is looking for you
and her soul is a corn-tassel kissing a south-west wind.

(The farm-boy whose face is the color of brick-dust,
   is calling the cows; he will form the letter X with
   crossed streams of milk from the teats; he will
   beat a tattoo on the bottom of a tin pail with X's
   of milk.)

I don't care who you are, man:
I know sons and daughters looking for you
And they are gray dust working toward star paths
And you see them from a garret window when you
   laugh
At your luck and murmur, " I don't care."

I don't care who you are, woman:
I know a man is looking for you
And his soul is a south-west wind kissing a corn-
   tassel.

(The kitchen girl on the farm is throwing oats to the
   chickens and the buff of their feathers says hello
   to the sunset's late maroon.)

I don't care who you are, woman:
I know sons and daughters looking for you
And they are next year's wheat or the year after
   hidden in the dark and loam.

My love is a yellow hammer spinning circles in Ohio,
   Indiana. My love is a redbird shooting flights
   in straight lines in Kentucky and Tennessee. My
   love is an early robin flaming an ember of copper

on her shoulders in March and April. My love
is a graybird living in the eaves of a Michigan
house all winter. Why is my love always a crying
thing of wings?

On the Indiana dunes, in the Mississippi marshes, I
    have asked: Is it only a fishbone on the beach?
Is it only a dog's jaw or a horse's skull whitening in
    the sun? Is the red heart of man only ashes?
    Is the flame of it all a white light switched off
    and the power house wires cut?

Why do the prairie roses answer every summer? Why
    do the changing repeating rains come back out
    of the salt sea wind-blown? Why do the stars
    keep their tracks? Why do the cradles of the
    sky rock new babies?

CADENZA

THE knees
   of this proud woman
are bone.

The elbows
   of this proud woman
are bone.

The summer-white stars
   and the winter-white stars
never stop circling
   around this proud woman.

The bones
   of this proud woman
answer the vibrations
   of the stars.

In summer
the stars speak deep thoughts
   In the winter
the stars repeat summer speeches.

The knees
   of this proud woman
know these thoughts
   and know these speeches
of the summer and winter stars.

MEMORANDA

THIS handful of grass, brown, says little. This quarter mile field of it, waving seeds ripening in the sun, is a lake of luminous firefly lavender.

. . . .

Prairie roses, two of them, climb down the sides of a road ditch. In the clear pool they find their faces along stiff knives of grass, and cat-tails who speak and keep thoughts in beaver brown.

. . . .

These gardens empty; these fields only flower ghosts; these yards with faces gone; leaves speaking as feet and skirts in slow dances to slow winds; I turn my head and say good-by to no one who hears; I pronounce a useless good-by.

POTOMAC TOWN IN FEBRUARY

THE bridge says: Come across, try me; see how good
I am.
The big rock in the river says: Look at me; learn
how to stand up.
The white water says: I go on; around, under, over,
I go on.
A kneeling, scraggly pine says: I am here yet; they
nearly got me last year.
A sliver of moon slides by on a high wind calling: I
know why; I'll see you to-morrow; I'll tell you
everything to-morrow.

BUFFALO DUSK

THE buffaloes are gone.
And those who saw the buffaloes are gone.
Those who saw the buffaloes by thousands and how
    they pawed the prairie sod into dust with their
    hoofs, their great heads down pawing on in a
    great pageant of dusk,
Those who saw the buffaloes are gone.
And the buffaloes are gone.

CORN HUT TALK

WRITE your wishes
    on the door
    and come in.

Stand outside
    in the pools of the harvest moon.

Bring in
    the handshake of the pumpkins.

There's a wish
    for every hazel nut?
There's a hope
    for every corn shock?
There's a kiss
    for every clumsy climbing shadow?

Clover and the bumblebees once,
high winds and November rain now.

Buy shoes
    for rough weather in November.
Buy shirts
    to sleep outdoors when May comes.

Buy me
something useless to remember you by.
Send me
a sumach leaf from an Illinois hill.

In the faces marching in the firelog flickers,
In the fire music of wood singing to winter,
Make my face march through the purple and ashes.
Make me one of the fire singers to winter.

BRANCHES

THE dancing girls here . . . after a long night of
    it . . .
The long beautiful night of the wind and rain in April,
The long night hanging down from the drooping
    branches of the top of a birch tree,
Swinging, swaying, to the wind for a partner, to the
    rain for a partner.
What is the humming, swishing thing they sing in
    the morning now?
The rain, the wind, the swishing whispers of the long
    slim curve so little and so dark on the western
    morning sky . . . these dancing girls here on an
    April early morning . . .
They have had a long cool beautiful night of it with
    their partners learning this year's song of April.

RUSTY CRIMSON

(*Christmas Day,* 1917)

THE five o'clock prairie sunset is a strong man going
to sleep after a long day in a cornfield.

The red dust of a rusty crimson is fixed with two
fingers of lavender. A hook of smoke, a woman's
nose in charcoal and . . . nothing.

The timberline turns in a cover of purple. A grain
elevator humps a shoulder. One steel star whisks
out a pointed fire. Moonlight comes on the
stubble.

. . . .

" Jesus in an Illinois barn early this morning, the
baby Jesus . . . in flannels . . ."

LETTER S

THE river is gold under a sunset of Illinois.
It is a molten gold someone pours and changes.
A woman mixing a wedding cake of butter and eggs
Knows what the sunset is pouring on the river here.
The river twists in a letter S.
    A gold S now speaks to the Illinois sky.

WEEDS

From the time of the early radishes
To the time of the standing corn
Sleepy Henry Hackerman hoes.

There are laws in the village against weeds.
The law says a weed is wrong and shall be killed.
The weeds say life is a white and lovely thing
And the weeds come on and on in irrepressible regiments.
Sleepy Henry Hackerman hoes; and the village law uttering a ban on weeds is unchangeable law.

NEW FARM TRACTOR

SNUB nose, the guts of twenty mules are in your
cylinders and transmission.

The rear axles hold the kick of twenty Missouri
jackasses.

It is in the records of the patent office and the ads
there is twenty horse power pull here.

The farm boy says hello to you instead of twenty
mules—he sings to you instead of ten span of
mules.

A bucket of oil and a can of grease is your hay and
oats.

Rain proof and fool proof they stable you anywhere
in the fields with the stars for a roof.

I carve a team of long ear mules on the steering wheel
—it's good-by now to leather reins and the songs
of the old mule skinners.

PODS

Pea pods cling to stems.
Neponset, the village,
Clings to the Burlington railway main line.
Terrible midnight limiteds roar through
Hauling sleepers to the Rockies and Sierras.
The earth is slightly shaken
And Neponset trembles slightly in its sleep.

HARVEST SUNSET

RED gold of pools,
Sunset furrows six o'clock,
And the farmer done in the fields
And the cows in the barns with bulging udders.

Take the cows and the farmer,
Take the barns and bulging udders.
Leave the red gold of pools
And sunset furrows six o'clock.
The farmer's wife is singing.
The farmer's boy is whistling.
I wash my hands in red gold of pools.

NIGHT'S NOTHINGS AGAIN

Who knows what I know
when I have asked the night questions
and the night has answered nothing
only the old answers?

Who picked a crimson cryptogram,
the tail light of a motor car turning a corner,
or the midnight sign of a chile con carne place,
or a man out of the ashes of false dawn muttering
    "hot-dog" to the night watchmen:
Is there a spieler who has spoken the word or taken
    the number of night's nothings? am I the spieler?
    or you?

Is there a tired head
the night has not fed and rested
and kept on its neck and shoulders?

Is there a wish
of man to woman
and woman to man
the night has not written
and signed its name under?

Does the night forget
as a woman forgets?
and remember
as a woman remembers?

Who gave the night
this head of hair,
this gipsy head
calling: Come-on?

Who gave the night anything at all
and asked the night questions
and was laughed at?

Who asked the night
for a long soft kiss
and lost the half-way lips?
who picked a red lamp in a mist?

Who saw the night
fold its Mona Lisa hands
and sit half-smiling, half-sad,
nothing at all,
and everything,
all the world?

Who saw the night
let down its hair
and shake its bare shoulders
and blow out the candles of the moon,
whispering, snickering,
cutting off the snicker . . and sobbing . .
out of pillow-wet kisses and tears?

Is the night woven of anything else
than the secret wishes of women,
the stretched empty arms of women?
the hair of women with stars and roses?

I asked the night these questions.
I heard the night asking me these questions.

I saw the night
put these whispered nothings
across the city dust and stones,
across a single yellow sunflower,
one stalk strong as a woman's wrist;

And the play of a light rain,
the jig-time folly of a light rain,
the creepers of a drizzle on the sidewalks
for the policemen and the railroad men,
for the home-goers and the homeless,
silver fans and funnels on the asphalt,
the many feet of a fog mist that crept away;

I saw the night
put these nothings across
and the night wind came saying: Come-on:
and the curve of sky swept off white clouds
and swept on white stars over Battery to Bronx,
scooped a sea of stars over Albany, Dobbs Ferry, Cape
     Horn, Constantinople.

I saw the night's mouth and lips
strange as a face next to mine on a pillow
and now I know . . . as I knew always . . .
the night is a lover of mine . . .
I know the night is . . . everything.
I know the night is . . . all the world.

I have seen gold lamps in a lagoon
play sleep and murmur
with never an eyelash,
never a glint of an eyelid,
quivering in the water-shadows.

A taxi whizzes by, an owl car clutters, passengers yawn
reading street signs, a bum on a park bench shifts,
another bum keeps his majesty of stone stillness,
the forty-foot split rocks of Central Park sleep
the sleep of stone whalebacks, the cornices of the
Metropolitan Art mutter their own nothings to the
men with rolled-up collars on the top of a bus:
Breaths of the sea salt Atlantic, breaths of two rivers,
and a heave of hawsers and smokestacks, the
swish of multiplied sloops and war dogs, the hesi-
tant hoo-hoo of coal boats: among these I listen
to Night calling:
I give you what money can never buy: all other lovers
change: all others go away and come back and go
away again:
I am the one you slept with last night.
I am the one you sleep with tonight and
tomorrow night.
I am the one whose passion kisses
keep your head wondering
and your lips aching
to sing one song
never sung before
at night's gipsy head
calling: Come-on.

These hands that slid to my neck and held me,
these fingers that told a story,
this gipsy head of hair calling: Come-on:
can anyone else come along now
and put across night's nothings again?

I have wanted kisses my heart stuttered at asking,
I have pounded at useless doors and called my people
     fools.
I have staggered alone in a winter dark making
     mumble songs
to the sting of a blizzard that clutched and swore.

    It was the night in my blood:
      open dreaming night,
      night of tireless sheet-steel blue:
    The hands of God washing something,
      feet of God walking somewhere.

PANELS

PANELS

The west window is a panel of marching onions.
Five new lilacs nod to the wind and fence boards.
The rain dry fence boards, the stained knot holes,
      heliograph a peace.
(How long ago the knee drifts here and a blizzard
      howling at the knot holes,
        whistling winter war drums?)

DAN

EARLY May, after cold rain the sun baffling cold wind.
Irish setter pup finds a corner near the cellar door,
            all sun and no wind,
Cuddling there he crosses forepaws and lays his skull
Sideways on this pillow, dozing in a half-sleep,
Browns of hazel nut, mahogany, rosewood, played off
                against each other on his paws
                and head.

WHIFFLETREE

Give me your anathema.
Speak new damnations on my head.
The evening mist in the hills is soft.
The boulders on the road say communion.
The farm dogs look out of their eyes and keep thoughts
    from the corn cribs.
Dirt of the reeling earth holds horseshoes.
The rings in the whiffletree count their secrets.
Come on, you.

MASCOTS

I WILL keep you and bring hands to hold you against
a great hunger.
I will run a spear in you for a great gladness to die
with.
I will stab you between the ribs of the left side with
a great love worth remembering.

THE SKYSCRAPER LOVES NIGHT

ONE by one lights of a skyscraper fling their checker-
ing cross work on the velvet gown of night.
I believe the skyscraper loves night as a woman and
brings her playthings she asks for, brings her a
velvet gown,
And loves the white of her shoulders hidden under
the dark feel of it all.

The masonry of steel looks to the night for somebody
it loves,
He is a little dizzy and almost dances . . . waiting
. . . dark . . .

NEVER BORN

THE time has gone by.
The child is dead.
The child was never even born.
Why go on? Why so much as begin?
How can we turn the clock back now
And not laugh at each other
As ashes laugh at ashes?

THIN STRIPS

In a jeweler's shop I saw a man beating
out thin sheets of gold. I heard a woman
laugh many years ago.

Under a peach tree I saw petals scattered
. . torn strips of a bride's dress. I heard
a woman laugh many years ago.

FIVE CENT BALLOONS

Pietro has twenty red and blue balloons on a string.
They flutter and dance pulling Pietro's arm.
A nickel apiece is what they sell for.

Wishing children tag Pietro's heels.

He sells out and goes the streets alone.

MY PEOPLE

My people are gray,
   pigeon gray, dawn gray, storm gray.
I call them beautiful,
   and I wonder where they are going.

SWIRL

A SWIRL in the air where your head was once, here.
You walked under this tree, spoke to a moon for me
I might almost stand here and believe you alive.

WISTFUL

Wishes left on your lips
The mark of their wings.
Regrets fly kites in your eyes.

BASKET

SPEAK, sir, and be wise.
Speak choosing your words, sir,
    like an old woman over a bushel
    of apples.

FIRE PAGES

I WILL read ashes for you, if you ask me.
I will look in the fire and tell you from the gray lashes
And out of the red and black tongues and stripes,
I will tell how fire comes
And how fire runs far as the sea.

FINISH

DEATH comes once, let it be easy.
Ring one bell for me once, let it go at that.
Or ring no bell at all, better yet.

Sing one song if I die.
Sing John Brown's Body or Shout All Over God's
    Heaven.
Or sing nothing at all, better yet.

Death comes once, let it be easy.

FOR YOU

THE peace of great doors be for you.
Wait at the knobs, at the panel oblongs.
Wait for the great hinges.

The peace of great churches be for you,
Where the players of loft pipe organs
Practice old lovely fragments, alone.

The peace of great books be for you,
Stains of pressed clover leaves on pages,
Bleach of the light of years held in leather.

The peace of great prairies be for you.
Listen among windplayers in cornfields,
The wind learning over its oldest music.

The peace of great seas be for you.
Wait on a hook of land, a rock footing
For you, wait in the salt wash.

The peace of great mountains be for you,
The sleep and the eyesight of eagles,
Sheet mist shadows and the long look across.

The peace of great hearts be for you,
Valves of the blood of the sun,
Pumps of the strongest wants we cry.

The peace of great silhouettes be for you,
Shadow dancers alive in your blood now,
Alive and crying, " Let us out, let us out."

The peace of great changes be for you.
Whisper, Oh beginners in the hills.
Tumble, Oh cubs—to-morrow belongs to you.

The peace of great loves be for you.
Rain, soak these roots; wind, shatter the dry rot.
Bars of sunlight, grips of the earth, hug these.

The peace of great ghosts be for you,
Phantoms of night-gray eyes, ready to go
To the fog-star dumps, to the fire-white doors.

Yes, the peace of great phantoms be for you,
Phantom iron men, mothers of bronze,
Keepers of the lean clean breeds.

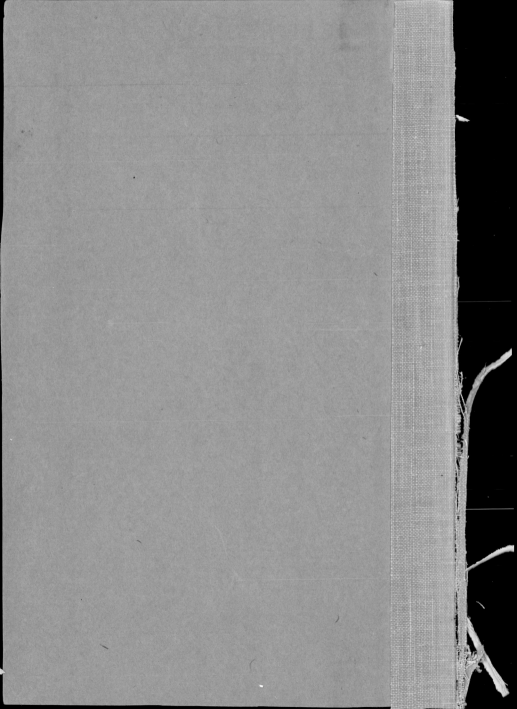